MW01232202

Ernest Hemingway

These and other titles are included in The Importance Of
biography series:

Alexander the Great
Muhammad Ali
Louis Armstrong
James Baldwin
Clara Barton
The Beatles
Napoleon Bonaparte
Julius Caesar
Rachel Carson
Charlie Chaplin
Charlemagne
Cesar Chavez
Winston Churchill
Cleopatra
Christopher Columbus
Hernando Cortes
Marie Curie
Charles Dickens
Emily Dickinson
Amelia Earhart
Thomas Edison
Albert Einstein
Duke Ellington
Dian Fossey
Anne Frank
Benjamin Franklin
Galileo Galilei
Emma Goldman
Jane Goodall
Martha Graham
Lorraine Hansberry
Stephen Hawking
Ernest Hemingway
Jim Henson
Adolf Hitler

Harry Houdini
Thomas Jefferson
Mother Jones
Chief Joseph
John F. Kennedy
Martin Luther King Jr.
Joe Louis
Malcolm X
Thurgood Marshall
Margaret Mead
Golda Meir
Michelangelo
Wolfgang Amadeus Mozart
John Muir
Sir Isaac Newton
Richard M. Nixon
Georgia O'Keeffe
Louis Pasteur
Pablo Picasso
Elvis Presley
Jackie Robinson
Norman Rockwell
Eleanor Roosevelt
Anwar Sadat
Margaret Sanger
Oskar Schindler
William Shakespeare
John Steinbeck
Tecumseh
Jim Thorpe
Mark Twain
Queen Victoria
Pancho Villa
H. G. Wells

Ernest Hemingway

by Paula Bryant Pratt

Lucent Books, P.O. Box 289011, San Diego, CA 92198-9011

Library of Congress Cataloging-in-Publication Data

Pratt, Paula Bryant, 1959–
    The importance of Ernest Hemingway / by Paula Bryant
      Pratt.
        p.   cm. — (The importance of)
    Includes bibliographical references (p.   ) and index.
    Summary: Discusses the life, work, and significance of the
  noted American writer, author of such works as "For Whom
  the Bell Tolls" and "The Old Man and the Sea."
    ISBN 1-56006-358-0 (lib. bdg. : alk. paper)
    1. Hemingway, Ernest, 1899–1961—Juvenile literature.
  2. Authors, American—20th century—Biography—Juvenile
  literature. [1. Hemingway, Ernest, 1899–1961. 2. Authors,
  American.]   I. Title.   II. Series.
  PS3515.E37Z75425   1999
  813'.52—dc21   98–37073
    [b]   CIP
                                                        AC

Copyright 1999 by Lucent Books, Inc., P.O. Box 289011,
San Diego, California, 92198-9011

Printed in the U.S.A.

Contents

Foreword

THE IMPORTANCE OF biography series deals with individuals who have made a unique contribution to history. The editors of the series have deliberately chosen to cast a wide net and include people from all fields of endeavor. Individuals from politics, music, art, literature, philosophy, science, sports, and religion are all represented. In addition, the editors did not restrict the series to individuals whose accomplishments have helped change the course of history. Of necessity, this criterion would have eliminated many whose contribution was great, though limited. Charles Darwin, for example, was responsible for radically altering the scientific view of the natural history of the world. His achievements continue to impact the study of science today. Others, such as Chief Joseph of the Nez Percé, played a pivotal role in the history of their own people. While Joseph's influence does not extend much beyond the Nez Percé, his nonviolent resistance to white expansion and his continuing role in protecting his tribe and his homeland remain an inspiration to all.

These biographies are more than factual chronicles. Each volume attempts to emphasize an individual's contributions both in his or her own time and for posterity. For example, the voyages of Christopher Columbus opened the way to European colonization of the New World. Unquestionably, his encounter with the New World brought monumental changes to both Europe and the Americas in his day. Today, however, the broader impact of Columbus's voyages is being critically scrutinized. *Christopher Columbus,* as well as every biography in The Importance Of series, includes and evaluates the most recent scholarship available on each subject.

Each author includes a wide variety of primary and secondary source quotations to document and substantiate his or her work. All quotes are footnoted to show readers exactly how and where biographers derive their information, as well as provide stepping-stones to further research. These quotations enliven the text by giving readers eyewitness views of the life and times of each individual covered in The Importance Of series.

Finally, each volume is enhanced by photographs, bibliographies, chronologies, and comprehensive indexes. For both the casual reader and the student engaged in research, The Importance Of biographies will be a fascinating adventure into the lives of people who have helped shape humanity's past and present, and who will continue to shape its future.

IMPORTANT DATES IN THE LIFE OF ERNEST HEMINGWAY

1899
Ernest Miller Hemingway born in Oak Park, Illinois, on July 21.

1917
Graduates from Oak Park High School. Works as a cub reporter for the *Kansas City Star* through April 1918.

1918
Joins the Red Cross ambulance unit during World War I. Wounded by mortar fragments near Fossalta di Piave, Italy.

1920
Freelance reporter for *Toronto Star*.

1921
Marries Elizabeth Hadley Richardson. Moves to Paris.

1921–1924
Reporter and foreign correspondent for the *Toronto Star*.

1923
Publishes first book, *Three Stories and Ten Poems*.

1924
Publishes *in our time* (Parisian edition).

1925
Publishes *In Our Time* (expanded U.S. edition).

1926
Publishes *The Torrents of Spring* and *The Sun Also Rises*.

1927
Divorces Hadley. Marries Pauline Pfeiffer. Publishes *Men Without Women*.

1929
Publishes *A Farewell to Arms*.

1932
Publishes *Death in the Afternoon*.

1933
Publishes *Winner Take Nothing*.

1935
Publishes *Green Hills of Africa*.

1937
Publishes *To Have and Have Not*.

1937–1939
Covers Spanish Civil War for North American Newspaper Alliance.

1938
Completes *The Spanish Earth*, *The Fifth Column*, and *The First Forty-Nine Stories*.

1940
Divorces Pauline. Marries Martha Gellhorn. Moves to Havana, Cuba. Publishes *For Whom the Bell Tolls*.

1946
Divorces Martha Gellhorn. Marries Mary Welsh Monks.

1950
Publishes *Across the River and into the Trees*.

1952
Publishes *The Old Man and the Sea*.

1953
Awarded the Pulitzer Prize for Fiction for *The Old Man and the Sea*.

1954
Awarded the Nobel Prize for Literature.

1961
Dies in Ketchum, Idaho, of self-inflicted gunshot wound, July 2.

A Private Battle

The respected American writer Ernest Miller Hemingway was born at the end of the nineteenth century. While still a young man, he rocketed to international prominence as one of the most talked-about authors of the twentieth century. His hair-raising adventures and outrageous personality made Hemingway himself as famous as his fiction.

Ernest Hemingway made an unforgettable impression on people. Dark-eyed and muscular with a flashing smile, he sparked with energy. He could be warm and witty when trying to impress someone, cold and crude when he was bored. He dressed for action, preferring sweatshirts and leather hunting vests to fancy suits. He bounced slightly when he walked, as if ready to pounce. He peppered his conversation with military slang, playful nicknames, and profanity. People who met him use contradictory terms to describe him—boastful, romantic, exuberant, insulting, phony, charming, inspiring.

His fame forced Hemingway to live his life in the public eye. In response, he deliberately took on many "tough-guy," traditionally masculine roles. He was a sportsman—

In addition to being a prolific writer and reporter, Hemingway was an avid outdoorsman and hunter. He is seen here on one of the many big-game hunting trips he took to Africa.

big-game hunter, boxer, deep-sea fisherman, bullfight fan. He was a wounded veteran of one war and an observant reporter of several others. Fiercely competitive, he was always poised to take on the world to defend his superiority.

The world was well aware of Hemingway's swaggering public personality. But he tried his best to hide his tortured private life. Only a handful of intimates caught glimpses of the author's ongoing battle against a serious illness—depression. In reality, depression continually threatened to topple him, even at the peaks of his popular success. While fending off repeated attacks of crippling sadness and despair, Hemingway stubbornly returned to his work, producing some of the finest modern American fiction.

In the course of this constant struggle to survive, Hemingway injected into his work the private demons that tormented him. He wrote of a world that was complicated and hostile. Within it, characters endure pain and hardship with varying degrees of courage and honor. The struggles of Hemingway's characters—the "lost" post–World War I young people of *The Sun Also Rises,* the disillusioned officer in *A Farewell to Arms,* the Cuban fisherman who refuses to give up his catch in *The Old Man and the Sea*—parallel Hemingway's own sense of the world and humanity's difficult place in it.

The intensity of Hemingway's personal struggle with despair gave his stories and novels a highly charged, emotional quality. That intensity, coupled with a clear, direct way of putting simple words together, made his writing style shockingly modern for its day. In fact, the writing style Hemingway pioneered was widely copied and influences authors to this day.

As he made clear in his life and work, Hemingway did not believe in giving up. After years of striving for excellence, he won the coveted Pulitzer and Nobel Prizes for his writing. Ultimately, however, he lost his battle with depression. Ernest Hemingway's suicide on July 2, 1961, stunned the world. The author's highly respected and highly readable work, however, lives on.

Chapter 1

Origins of a Writer

Five-year-old Ernest Hemingway was a hero. All by himself, he had stopped a runaway horse in mid-gallop. Back home, he reported the victory to his grandfather in detail. Ernest Hall listened in amazement. It couldn't have happened, but Ernest told his tale so convincingly, it seemed almost real. Hall said, "This boy is going to be

Ernest demonstrated his story-telling ability at an early age when he related a tale of a runaway horse to his grandfather, Ernest Hall.

heard from some day. If he uses his imagination for good purposes, he'll be famous, but if he starts the wrong way, with all his energy, he'll end up in jail."[1] Ernest's mother made a mental note of her father's words and did what she could to channel her son's energy in the right direction.

Meanwhile, Ernest continued to let his imagination run wild, and his skill at telling impressive stories did not lead to jail, after all. Instead, his talent brought him worldwide recognition as an important author.

Born on July 21, 1899, in Oak Park, Illinois, near Chicago, Ernest was the second of six children. At the turn of the twentieth century, doctors made house calls in horse-drawn carts, women wore stockings and long skirts on outings to the beach, and bystanders yelled "Get a horse!" at drivers navigating automobiles along bumpy paths. Until he was six years old, Ernest lived in the comfortable three-story Victorian-style house built by his grandfather Ernest Hall. The house had one of the first telephones in town and a circular tower where Ernest's father, a doctor, stored his medical specimens—including an appendix in a jar and a skeleton called Susie Bone-a-part.

Ernest's father, Clarence Hemingway, was just starting his medical career when he married Grace Hall. They were magnetic people whose charm and enthusiasm attracted admirers. And their older son shared many of their positive qualities, including his mother's creativity. Ernest's sister Sunny recalled, "My mother was hard to get along with at times, since she held strong views. But my father adored her. When she entered a room everyone took note of her. She was the buoyant, creative one in the family, much like Ernie."[2]

Putting Talent to Work

Grace, a talented singer, musician, and composer, encouraged her children to express themselves. She herself did not hold back when she wanted to make her presence known. As a child of seven, Grace had gone blind for six months after coming down with scarlet fever. Before she regained her sight, she taught herself to play the family organ by feeling the keys. At twelve, she shocked her neighbors by putting on her brother's long pants and going for a wild ride on his newfangled bicycle, back when the contraption's front wheel was several feet high and merely pedaling one was dangerous. By the time Grace was a young woman, the Metropolitan Opera was interested in her work, and she stood on the threshold of a professional opera career. But in the meantime, she attracted the admiration of an equally strong personality, Clarence Hemingway. He persuaded her to marry him.

Grace didn't become a diva, but she never abandoned music. In a day when most married women did not hold regular jobs, she earned a substantial amount of money to add to her husband's earnings as a doctor. She taught voice, sang in concerts, and sold original song lyrics and mu-

Ernest's mother, Grace (seen here with her father, Ernest Hall), was a talented musician and singer. She encouraged her son's creativity when he was a child.

sical accompaniments for publication. Ernest grew up in an atmosphere where creative work was respected and nurtured, even if it meant losing sleep. His older sister, Marcelline, recalls: "Often I would wake up in the night, sometimes long after midnight, hearing the piano. I knew it was Mother working on some composition which had come to her in her sleep. She told us that if she dreamed a melody and got right up and played it out on the piano immediately, she could remember it the next day, to write it down."[3]

Grace was an affectionate mother who recorded her son Ernest's funny childhood sayings and encouraged him to shout, "'Fraid of nothing!" But she was also an unconventional woman for her time. She not only valued her privacy, she insisted upon having it, closing herself off in the music room to practice for hours. She rarely cooked or cleaned house, preferring to pay others out of her music earnings to do such chores for the family. The enterprising, unapologetic way she put her talent to work impressed Ernest. But Grace's outspokenness when she felt her son needed correction often caused them to clash as he grew older.

Self-Starters

Ernest's father, Clarence, known as Ed, was as adventurous and energetic as his wife, but he was also quite strict. He did not approve of card-playing, dancing, or drinking alcohol. He saw to it that the family attended the local Congregational church regularly. And although he was caring, he was a harsh disciplinarian, whipping his children when they disobeyed, then ordering them to kneel and pray for God's forgiveness. Ernest's father expected his family and friends to hold to high standards of behavior, and demanded the same exacting moral conduct from himself. As an adult, Ernest himself would show the same rigid attitudes toward himself and others.

A tall, burly man who had been a football player at Oberlin College, Ed Hemingway loved the outdoors and took pleasure in opening its secrets to others. He organized a nature club for Oak Park's young people, taking twenty or so boys and girls at a time on long hikes along the banks of the Des Plaines River, stopping to inspect birds' nests, rare plants, foxholes, and woodchuck burrows. He taught the club to shake the dirt from freshly plucked wild onions and eat them in a sandwich with bread and butter. In addition to his energy, Ernest's appreciation of nature and

his keen powers of observation were traits he shared with his father. The young boy's growing intimacy with nature and these leisurely opportunities to study it at close range would end up helping him later in his writing career.

As much as his wife, Grace, was a creative thinker, Ed Hemingway was a man of action. He could never stand to be idle, let alone understand why his children might

Ernest's father, Clarence, was a doctor and a strict disciplinarian. Though he sometimes had an explosive temper, Clarence cultivated Ernest's deep love for the outdoors.

sometimes prefer to sit and read when they could be working on something constructive. When he was not on his doctor's rounds, he was always puttering on some project, usually with a group of his children surrounding him, teaching them to can fruit, make candles, chop wood, or otherwise make themselves useful. Ed Hemingway encouraged his children to be self-starters, to make an impact on the outside world. His first son was destined to make a huge impact.

Walloon Lake

The Hemingways escaped every summer to their cottage at Walloon Lake, Michigan, about nine miles from Petoskey, the nearest town. The cottage was so isolated that when the family needed supplies, they hung an old white sheet from the porch railing to signal passing boats toward their dock. At Walloon Lake, Ernest and his brothers and sisters learned to swim and to shoot air rifles. They went fishing and ate their catch outside on the porch. Ernest slept in a tent in the backyard. His pals from town often came to the lake to sleep over. Late at night, by a lantern's glow, Ernest silently read horror stories and adventure novels in his tent under a curtain of mosquito netting. When he had grown up and become a writer, Ernest remembered this annual release from the chains of small-town life and used it in his work. He drew upon many of the new people and places he came to know, including the lumberjacks and Ottawa Indians who worked in the area's logging camps.

The open spaces and relaxed atmosphere at Walloon Lake brought out the storyteller in Ernest. His friend Lew Clarahan recalled that on a long hike in 1915, Ernest "made up startling stories and situa-

Ernest's Strict Father

This passage from Bernice Kert's The Hemingway Women *describes Ed Hemingway's severity when disciplining his children. The punishments from Ernest's moody and unpredictable father may have affected his later life and work.*

"Rules of behavior within the household were established by Ed Hemingway. He enforced the Sabbath strictly—no play or games, no visiting with friends, and prayers and church attendance were mandatory. For infractions of behavior he used the razor strop liberally. His temper could flare up in a second. It was the unpredictability of his disapproval more than the punishment that was sometimes hard on the juvenile wrongdoers. . . . Washing out mouths with bitter-tasting soap was routine for objectionable remarks."

Ernest's family spent many of their summers at their vacation house on Walloon Lake in a secluded part of Michigan. The wilderness setting enhanced Hemingway's creative side.

tions and shouted them to the trees."[4] The teenager joined his father when Ed tended to workers at the logging camps and their families, then turned his imaginings about what he witnessed into melodrama. One day, he scribbled this dramatic idea for a story in his journal: "Rainy night. Tough looking lumberjack. Young Indian girl. Kills self and girl."[5]

A Love of Drama

Ernest had always had a knack for language, making up stories and silly nicknames for his family and friends. In high school, his instructors often read his compositions out loud to his classmates. He expressed his ideas with humor and enthusiasm, catching people's attention with the forceful personality behind his words. Lew Clarahan recalls that even the way Ernest spoke to his friends showed his potential as a writer:

> He loved drama and would exaggerate any little incident, possibly on occasion offending someone who did not make the proper allowances. When he had a good tale to tell, he liked to back one into a corner, while giving soft punches to retain attention as he told the story. . . . His love of drama . . . was of course a distinct advantage to him as a writer.[6]

By the time he became a popular up- perclassman at Oak Park High School, Er- nest was a full-fledged author. He dashed off breezy articles on sports and school events for the student newspaper, *Trapeze.* Fellow students called him "Ring Lardner," after a popular newspaper columnist of the day. He also wrote several fiction sto- ries for *Tabula,* the school literary maga- zine. The first to appear was a gory tale of murder and suicide in the frigid north woods. A second story dealt with a rigged boxing match.

Ernest's early attempts at writing brought him the attention he thrived on. And all his practice on the student news- paper and literary magazine made the words come easily. Concentrating enough to stick with tasks that did not come easily, however, was a skill he was still learning. According to his sister Marcelline, "Ernest, who could be a most charming compan- ion, could also be completely indifferent to . . . any responsibilities which did not appeal to him."[7] There were plenty of things the teenage Ernest would rather not do. Although his mother hoped that Ernest might develop into a musician and insisted that he practice the cello daily, he often faked obedience by closing the mu- sic room door and sawing mechanically back and forth on the strings while simul- taneously reading from a favorite book he had smuggled in with him.

Most of the time, Ernest stayed out of trouble because he and his brothers and sisters were afraid of a whipping from their father—or a lick from a hairbrush from their mother—if they broke a family rule. The Hemingways tried to teach their chil- dren the consequences of their actions. Once Ed ordered Ernest and a friend to cook and eat a porcupine they had killed,

because it was a family rule never to shoot animals that would not be used for food. Grace and Ed themselves were models of good discipline and responsibility in the way they dedicated themselves to their work, family, and community.

Consequences

The Hemingways' concern that their chil- dren do the right thing, however, some- times caused them to be overprotective. Before Ernest graduated from high school, his parents did not allow him a lot of lee- way to make his own decisions or to learn what it was like to be responsible for him- self. The decisions he made could be bad ones, like the time he impulsively shot a rare blue heron while on an outing with his little sister Sunny, thinking it might look good in the school museum.

An outraged witness—the game war- den's son—reported him for breaking the law. Panicking, Ernest's first response was to hide in the woods. His father persuaded Ernest to show up in court, where he got off with a $15 fine—a lot of money in those days. Released from the fear of worse punishment, Ernest bragged about how he had escaped the warden's clutches until Ed reminded him that it would have been cheaper to obey the game laws in the first place.

Cub Reporter

Grace and Ed wanted their son to go to college, but after graduating from high school in 1917, Ernest wanted to learn about life outside of school, away from his quiet hometown and dominating parents. An uncle offered to get him a job as a cub reporter on the *Kansas City Star*. The newspaper needed to hire people to replace reporters who had joined the fighting overseas. The terrible global conflict, begun in 1914, would cause the worst loss of human life the world had yet seen, recorded in history as World War I. Ernest was interested in taking on a reporting job. The paper wanted to hire him, but a position would not be open until October. Pacing restlessly on the brink of freedom, Ernest spent the summer helping with outdoor chores. Feeling that he was too old to stay at home, he nevertheless behaved childishly, often arguing with his parents, then refusing to speak to them for long periods.

In mid-October, Ernest boarded a train for Kansas City. In 1917, the *Star*'s second-floor newsroom was a sea of desks, swarming with reporters and editors yelling above the clatter of typewriters. Ernest was assigned three "beats," or areas to write about—the police station, Union Station (a train terminal), and the local hospital. Ernest's absorption in his new role as a reporter sometimes got him into trouble. When he went out scouting for news, he often forgot to let his editor know where he could be reached.

Ernest showed other signs of taking his first real job very seriously. In the newsroom, Ernest was full of questions for his fellow reporters about the best way to tell a news story. And he devoured the *Star*'s stylebook, which gave these reporting tips: "Use short sentences. Use short first paragraphs. Use vigorous English, not forgetting to strive for smoothness. Be positive, not negative."[8] Now that he had latched

onto a pursuit that truly interested him, Ernest was showing the drive, persistence, and creativity his parents had encouraged all along.

Writer in Training

Newly dedicated to learning everything about the craft of writing, Ernest found his first job to be the perfect environment for his ambitious goal. Working as a cub reporter provided the ideal training ground. According to literary critic Joseph M. Flora, "He would in a very short time develop a distinctive prose style—praised as muscular, lean, efficient. [The] brief apprenticeship . . . on the *Kansas City Star* helped him toward that end, teaching him economy and directness . . . newspaper training had helped to sharpen his skills of observation and to form his style."[9] In the clatter and confusion of the *Star*'s newsroom, Ernest first experimented with the short sentences, powerful delivery, and attention to detail that marked his later fiction writing.

There was a lot to take in. Dramas unfolded daily. The young reporter found plenty of action at Kansas City's General Hospital. In January 1918, Ernest wrote about the hospital night shift, a time when near-dead patients were rushed in by ambulance, wounded in street-fight stabbings and beatings:

> When "George" comes in on the soiled, bloody stretcher and the rags are stripped off and his naked, broken body lies on the white table in the glare of the surgeon's light, and he dangles on a little thread of life, while the physicians struggle grimly, it is

"Mix War, Art And Dancing"

The full-length version of this article was originally published in the Kansas City Star *on April 21, 1918, when Hemingway was only eighteen. He won much praise from his colleagues at the paper for its simultaneous sensitivity and lack of sentiment. The story is extracted from* Ernest Hemingway, Cub Reporter, *edited by Matthew J. Bruccoli.*

"Outside a woman walked along the wet street-lamp lit sidewalk through the sleet and snow.

Inside in the Fine Arts Institute on the sixth floor of the Y.W.C.A. Building, 1020 McGee Street, a merry crowd of soldiers from Camp Funston and Fort Leavenworth fox trotted and one-stepped with girls from the Fine Arts School while a sober faced young man pounded out the latest jazz music as he watched the moving figures. . . . Three men from Funston were wandering arm in arm along the wall looking at the exhibition of paintings by Kansas City artists. The piano player stopped. The dancers clapped and cheered and he swung into The Long, Long Trail Awinding. An infantry corporal, dancing with a swift moving girl in a red dress, bent his head close to hers and confided something about a girl in Chautauqua, Kas. . . .

The music stopped again and the solemn pianist rose from his stool and walked out into the hall for a drink.

A crowd of men rushed up to the girl in the red dress to plead for the next dance. Outside the woman walked along the wet lamp lit sidewalk.

It was the first dance for soldiers to be given under the auspices of the War Camp Community Service. Forty girls of the art school, chaperoned by Miss Winifred Sexton, secretary of the school and Mrs. J. F. Binnie were the hostesses. . . . Posters made by the girl students were put up at Leavenworth and on the interurban trains. . . .

The pianist took his seat again and the soldiers made a dash for partners. In the intermission the soldiers drank to the girl in fruit punch. The girl in red, surrounded by a crowd of men in olive drab, seated herself at the piano, the men and the girls gathered around and sang until midnight. The elevator had stopped running and so the jolly crowd bunched down the six flights of stairs and rushed waiting motor cars. After the last car had gone, the woman walked along the wet sidewalk through the sleet and looked up at the dark windows of the sixth floor."

all in the night's work, whether the thread snaps or whether it holds so that George can fight on and work and play.[10]

All his life, Ernest had been exposed to death as he watched his father battling it on his medical rounds. But now that the *Star* had given him the task to write about life and death on a daily basis, the young reporter was forced to think about what these enormous issues meant to him. Writing for the *Star* was a way for Ernest to find out what he really thought and felt and to communicate it to readers in a way that moved them to think and feel, too. He was beginning to find a voice.

Ernest Enlists

As focused as Ernest was on the challenge of newspaper work, he was well aware of the tense drama unfolding overseas. Enlisting in the military was an issue uppermost in every young man's mind. The bloody international battle with Germany had started in 1914 with two pistol shots. It was fast becoming the costliest conflict—both in defense dollars and in human lives—that the globe had yet endured. Later, Ernest would write about a generation's loss of innocence as a result of that war. But at the time, his only thought was to serve his country without hesitation. Because of weak vision in his left eye, he didn't see well enough to enlist in a fighting unit. In spite of that disappointment, Ernest was ready to go and do what he could.

His worried parents were relieved that their first son would be joining the Red Cross ambulance unit, rather than actually fighting. Ernest landed in Schio, Italy, in June 1918. Italy was a U.S. ally. Although Ernest started out as a driver, his dedication to serving his country and his desire to observe everything he could about life prompted him to volunteer for the Red Cross "rolling canteen unit." This put him in a more dangerous position than ambulance driving because he would be distributing coffee, cigarettes, and chocolate to Italian soldiers at the front lines, right in the middle of the fighting.

On the night of July 8, about a month after he arrived in Italy, as Ernest was handing a candy bar to a soldier at the front in Fossalta di Piave, the Austrian army lobbed a trench mortar shell—a gallon can filled with explosives—into the area. The bomb blew up and Ernest's legs were peppered by more than two hundred shell fragments. One soldier was killed in the blast, others were seriously hurt. Stunned and numb, Ernest remembered swinging a wounded man over his shoulder and struggling toward the first-aid dugout. As he trudged forward, Ernest was hit a second time by machine-gun fire, recalling that it felt like being struck on the leg by a frozen snowball. He ended up in the American Red Cross Hospital in Milan. There, as he recovered from his wounds, he learned that the Italian command had chosen him for its Silver Medal of Valor.

Ernest and Agnes

At the hospital in Milan, all the nurses flirted with the handsome nineteen-year-old war hero, especially a tall, slim American nurse named Agnes von Kurowsky. She was six years older and called him

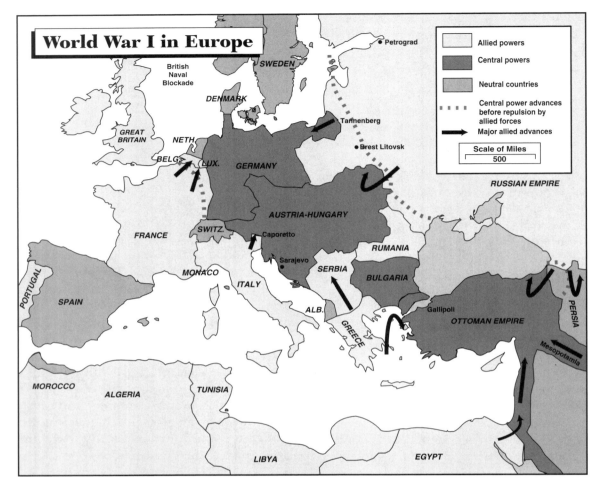

World War I in Europe

Allied powers

Central powers

Neutral countries

Central power advances before repulsion by allied forces

Major allied advances

Scale of Miles
500

Petrograd

SWEDEN

British Naval Blockade

DENMARK

GREAT BRITAIN

NETH.

BELG.

LUX.

GERMANY

Tannenberg

Brest Litovsk

RUSSIAN EMPIRE

FRANCE

SWITZ.

AUSTRIA-HUNGARY

Caporetto

RUMANIA

Sarajevo

SERBIA

BULGARIA

MONACO

ITALY

ALB.

GREECE

Gallipoli

OTTOMAN EMPIRE

PERSIA

Mesopotamia

PORTUGAL

SPAIN

MOROCCO

ALGERIA

TUNISIA

LIBYA

EGYPT

"Kid." Ernest fell in love with her. Throughout the months he spent healing in the hospital, Ernest could think of only one thing—Agnes. Agnes felt his attraction to her, and she wasn't sure what to do about it. An entry in her diary reveals that she liked him, too. "Ernest Hemingway is getting earnest. He was talking last night of what might be if he was 26–28. In some ways, at some times, wish very much that he was. He is adorable & we are very congenial in every way. I'm getting so confused in my heart & mind I don't know how I'll end up." [11]

Although Agnes encouraged his attentions, her patient's moodiness and controlling nature worried her. She wrote in her diary: "I am sorry to say the Kid has a jealous disposition. Every time I try to tease him I'm made sorry for it after, as he goes off at a tangent, without waiting to find out for sure." [12]

Ernest escorted Agnes on dates around Milan, beginning to feel at home in the cosmopolitan city as he hobbled around on crutches and later with a cane. While he enjoyed the attention he was getting as a result of his wounds, both from the pretty nurse and from his war buddies, he didn't really think of himself as a hero. He found time in October to write a letter to his parents that showed his new thoughtfulness, as well as his old tendency toward melodrama:

> There are no heroes in this war . . . all the heroes are dead. . . . When a mother brings a son into the world she must know that some day the son will die, and the mother of a man that has died for his country should be the proudest woman in the world, and the happiest. And how much better to die in all the happy period of undisillusioned youth, to go out in a blaze of light, than to have your body worn out and old and illusions shattered.[13]

The war was officially over on what became known as Armistice Day—November 11, 1918. Ernest and Agnes had been discussing marriage. She was willing to consider the idea, but she had plenty of doubts about Ernest's immaturity, bad temper, and dark moods. Furthermore, the young woman loved nursing and hesitated to give it up to become a wife—in those days married women rarely kept their careers. But Ernest himself had no doubts. The nineteen-year-old war veteran returned home to Oak Park in January 1919 believing that he and Agnes von Kurowsky would soon reunite and marry. As he lay in bed, his wounded legs aching, he wrote her dozens of letters. To remind him of Italy, he kept his red, green, and yellow Red Cross blanket spread over him in bed.

Agnes von Kurowsky was a nurse who tended to nineteen-year-old Hemingway after he was wounded in World War I. Hemingway fell in love with Agnes, who was six years his senior.

Rejection

Back in Italy, however, Agnes had decided that marrying Ernest would be a mistake. She began dating an Italian officer, an older man who suddenly seemed more appealing than a young man without an established career. In a letter dated March 7, 1919, Agnes broke up with Ernest, writing, "I am still very fond of you, but, it is more as a mother than as a sweetheart."[14]

According to Ernest's older sister, Marcelline, in her memoir, Ernest had been watching the mailbox constantly, edgy with suspense. After he read Agnes's shattering letter, Ernest went to bed and stayed there for several days, barely moving, his face to the wall. His family was worried. Medicine didn't seem to help. Ernest's grief at Agnes's rejection—news he did not share with his family at first—had made him sick. The physical problems were caused by his despairing thoughts and confused feelings, a condition known as depression. This crushing depression was a signpost in Ernest's life. It marked the first of many similar periods of despair and self-doubt that he was to battle for the rest of his life.

Depressed people are sad, but they are often angry as well, reacting to situations they feel they cannot control. Ernest was definitely angry as well as sorrowful at the way his hopes for marriage had crumbled. He wrote a friend about the rejection, ranting unfairly that he wished Agnes would fall down and break her front teeth. Ernest had loved Agnes with his whole heart. Her rejection had nearly leveled him. He recovered from the blow, but he

Americans celebrate the end of World War I. When Hemingway returned from Europe he received a letter from Agnes, ending their relationship. The bad news sent him into such a deep depression that he could not get out of bed for several days.

never forgot it, later injecting his powerful memories of Agnes into his World War I novel, *A Farewell to Arms*.

Hometown Hero

Meanwhile, the return of the young war hero caused a stir in his hometown. Twice, in February and March, Ernest was invited to speak at Oak Park High School about his adventures on the Italian front. Most of Ernest's friends who had returned from the war had taken jobs or returned to college. Because he was still recuperating, Ernest had to stay close to home and often got lonely. Speaking to the younger kids at his old school relieved his isolation and fed his ego. His former teacher Frank J. Platt recalled listening to him speak to a group of students:

> As he related the climax of his adventure, he produced his brown uniform . . . and passed [it] out with an invitation to count the bullet holes in the riddled garments. It was a most amusing sight to see forty high school boys, who had known him as an upperclassman, examining with infinite care the deadly rents in his clothes. There was some laughter, but there was an undertone feeling as to what war can mean to a man. This was a proud warrior's return, showing the dents in his shield.[15]

After his quick growing up overseas, Oak Park was anticlimactic for Ernest. He gave Marcelline some brotherly advice about the value of taking risks: "Don't be afraid to taste all the other things in life that aren't here in Oak Park. . . . Sometimes I think we only half live over here."[16]

Though Hemingway was a hero in his hometown, he found life in Oak Park boring after experiencing the excitement of wartime Europe. He spent his next few years drifting in Michigan and Canada.

For a while, the war veteran gave himself time to enjoy life, drifting aimlessly from a rooming house in Petoskey, Michigan, where he tried to write magazine fiction, to Toronto, Canada, where he baby-sat for a wealthy couple's young son. In Canada, he hooked up with the Toronto newspaper, also called the *Star*, and began freelancing for them. It was good experience, but the money was not enough to support him.

Leaving the Nest

By the summer of 1920, Ernest's parents were unhappy with their son's lack of initiative in getting a steady job. They were even more disappointed when he announced his plans to voyage to the Orient with three male friends. He would work as a sailor to pay his fare, he told his parents. All he needed from them was money for a passport and train fare to San Francisco. They refused to lend him the money, and he had to drop the idea. Ernest's scheme seemed self-centered and unrealistic at a time when the Hemingways were saving money to send Ernest's younger sister Ursula to college. Grace and the children were living in the cottage at Walloon Lake alone while Ed stayed behind in Chicago to work. Ernest agreed to help out at the cottage with the heavy chores his father usually did. But he didn't keep his promise, showing up only for meals then disappearing again to go fishing, ignoring his mother's attempts to discuss finances with him. He was now fully recovered from his wounds and had been out of work for months. Ernest was tired of being treated like a wayward child, but he had not yet demonstrated to his parents that he was a man of responsibility.

In frustration, Grace wrote him a stinging letter, telling him that he was irresponsible and ungrateful. She then issued an ultimatum—he need not bother to return home until he got a job. According to biographer Bernice Kert, Ernest's mother may have been overreacting to her son because they had so many personality traits in common: "It is possible that Grace was seeing some of her own undesirable traits in Ernest—his craving for excitement and romance, his tendency to exaggerate his experiences, his need to have things his own way."[17]

Chicago

Ernest, who took any criticism badly, was hurt and angry, but the blowup seemed to clear the air. Ernest moved in with Y. Kenley Smith, his friend Bill Smith's brother, and his wife. The couple lived in downtown Chicago. Ernest had accepted a job in the city as an editorial assistant for *Cooperative Commonwealth* magazine. Although he was not being paid to write stories, the young writer did not give up on his fiction writing while in Chicago. Instead, his approach to writing became more disciplined. During his stay in the city, Ernest worked on perfecting a unique way of seeing and expressing emotion, which he described later, saying that he

> was searching for the unnoticed things that made emotions such as the way an outfielder tossed his glove without looking back to where it fell, the squeak of resin on canvas under a fighter's flat-soled gym shoes . . . and other things I noted as a painter sketches. . . . Those were the things which moved you before you knew the story.[18]

Already his approach to writing had changed drastically from his high school days, when he tried to inspire horror or awe in his readers with heavy-handed, obvious events and manipulative language. His new approach of affecting readers' emotions with the simple creation of a telling detail—like the squeak of a prizefighter's shoes—was more subtle and potentially much more powerful.

In addition to finding new maturity in Chicago, in both his personal life and his writing, Ernest found his future wife, Elizabeth Hadley Richardson.

Hadley

Red-haired Hadley was eight years older than Ernest and had led a sheltered life taking care of her ill mother. Her mother had died, and at twenty-nine, Hadley was ready to start living life rather than hiding from it. Ernest and Hadley met at the regular Sunday get-togethers for friends hosted by the Smiths. Ernest fell in love with her auburn hair, her good nature, and her open appreciation of him. Ernest nicknamed Had-

ley "Hash Brown." She was a down-to-earth, unspoiled young woman. Ernest was impressed with the cheerful, matter-of-fact way she put up with a hurt ankle that was so swollen she had to wear a red felt slipper instead of a shoe to accompany Ernest on a date to a football game at the university. Ernest later told his sister Marcelline that Hash was "a real sport."

Ernest and Hadley communicated well, confiding both their simplest daily activities and their deepest longings to one another. Hadley knew how to reassure Ernest and make him feel important without flattering him. Ernest took Hadley home to meet his family. On September 3, 1921, Ernest and Hadley were married. According to Marcelline Hemingway Sanford, the marriage had her parents' full approval. In fact, they

While working for a magazine in Chicago, Ernest met Elizabeth Hadley Richardson. He found himself very attracted to her auburn hair and her down-to-earth manner. The two were married in September 1921.

were relieved: "They loved Hadley and they felt sure that Ernest would stick to a job now that he had such a wonderful wife."[19]

A Place for a Serious Writer

Hadley received a small income from two trust fund accounts, one from her late mother and one from her late grandfather. She was excited about using it to help support her young husband's writing career. They discussed moving to Italy with the money. But a friend of a friend, Sherwood Anderson, advised them to go to Paris. Anderson, in his forties, was well known as the author of an acclaimed best-selling novel, *Winesburg, Ohio*. Ernest wanted to be like Anderson some day, making a living writing fiction. Many important American writers and artists were already living in Paris on the Left Bank of the Seine River, free from the stuffy atmosphere of middle-class America. Paris was the place for a serious writer, Anderson insisted. Ernest could earn extra money writing articles on the European scene for the *Toronto Star,* Anderson suggested. The newlyweds, ready for adventure, were convinced.

Sherwood Anderson wrote letters introducing Ernest to some of his influential friends in Paris. He described Ernest as a fine newspaperman whose talent would take him far beyond journalism. Anderson's flattering prophecy would prove truer than he knew—the Hemingways' decision to take Anderson's advice and move to Paris played a big part in transforming the brash, buoyant twenty-two-year-old into one of the most famous and respected novelists of his generation.

2 Writer First

Paris in the 1920s teemed with artists and writers of every nationality. People were dizzy with relief that the threat of world war had lifted. They shared the feeling that an exciting new way of life, unchained by old rules, was on the horizon. That carefree attitude fueled the daring, experimental work of painters and writers who mingled in the Left Bank district of Paris, trading ideas and inventing new styles of expression. The festival atmosphere was distracting—even the Hemingways' tiny apartment was next door to a rowdy dance hall—but Hemingway had come to Paris to write. In his seven years there, he concentrated on little else.

Alone with a Notebook

One of Hemingway's first commitments to his craft was finding a place to write in solitude. He was determined to focus on his work until he produced an important story or novel, something worthy of the challenge he had set himself by moving to Paris in the first place. Like many of the

In the early 1920s, a friend had recommended that Hemingway and his wife move to Paris. Many American writers and artists were living and working on the Left Bank of the Seine River, and Hemingway thought it would be a good atmosphere for writing.

city's aspiring authors, Hemingway escaped the damp chill that first winter in one of the Left Bank's popular cafés. Bundled in a coat and a beret, he drank coffee and scribbled observations about people around him. But to truly concentrate he needed more privacy.

American dollars went a long way in Paris after the war. Although their combined income from Ernest's freelance journalism and Hadley's trust funds was small, the couple saved enough to pay for extras, including skiing trips to Switzerland and a housekeeper. The Hemingways decided to set aside some money to rent a room where Ernest could write.

Hemingway climbed the steep stairs to his hotel room "office" each morning and got to work. Writing fiction had been an entertaining game. In Paris, he treated it as serious business. In hope of improving the quality of his work, he experimented with slowing the flow of the words that had always come easily to him. He narrowed his goals, concentrating on writing fine sentences and paragraphs, trying to make each word strong and clear. In those first months in Paris, Hemingway crossed out as many words as he wrote. Decades later, he still remembered the pep talks he gave himself when he was tempted to quit:

> I would stand and look out over the roofs of Paris and think, "Do not worry. You have always written before and you will write now. All you have to do is write one true sentence. Write the truest sentence that you know." So finally I would write one true sentence, and then go on from there. It was easy then because there was always one true sentence that I knew or had seen or had heard someone say.[20]

Hemingway had started to think of good writing as writing that told the truth. In the Paris years, he dedicated himself to becoming a writer whose words were as honest as he could make them. But as motivated as he was, he had not yet come up with a satisfying method for making his voice ring true. He was determined to find one.

Foreign Correspondent

Writing about postwar Europe for the *Toronto Star* helped Hemingway shape his fiction writing. The huge amount of articles he produced challenged him to write as forcefully as he could, as fast as he could. There was no time to stop and think about the perfect place for a clever expression or a comma. And because he wired his stories to the newspaper by telegraph, Hemingway had to get to the point quickly. That helped tighten his fiction writing, comments literary critic Joseph M. Flora: "His assignment was not to report hard news, but to write human interest accounts, which he would wire in 'cablese,' an abbreviated style that challenged the young Hemingway to transmit his ideas using a minimum number of words."[21] The writing style Hemingway became famous for used a small number of words to talk about big ideas and emotions. Like readers of a telegram, Hemingway's readers understand that there is a larger message lurking behind his simple, clipped sentences.

From his Parisian home base, Hemingway flooded the *Toronto Star* with articles on topics as different as Swiss tourism and the election of Pope Pius XI at the Vatican. Since he could not achieve his goal of becoming a great novelist overnight, journal-

Reporting His Feelings

In his introduction to a collection of Ernest Hemingway's journalism, editor William White explained that the creative writer and keen observer in Hemingway made his reporting unique. From By-Line: Ernest Hemingway *by Ernest Hemingway, edited by William White.*

"As a reporter and foreign correspondent . . . Hemingway soaked up persons and places and life like a sponge: these were to become matter for his short stories and novels. His use of this material, however, sets him apart from other creative writers who, as he himself says, made their living as journalists, learning their trade, writing against deadlines, writing to make stuff timely rather than permanent. Hemingway . . . was always the creative writer: he used his material to suit his imaginative purposes. This does not mean he was not a good reporter, for he showed a grasp of politics and economics, was an amazing observer, and knew how to dig for information. But his craft was the craft of fiction, not factual reporting. And though he wrote as he saw things, his writing shows most vividly how he *felt* about what he saw."

---

ism was the next best way for Hemingway to support himself and Hadley while continuing to build his reputation as a writer. In the fall of 1922, pleased with his work, the *Star* assigned Hemingway to travel to the Middle East to cover the war between Greece and Turkey. The situation was dangerous. Hadley asked him to turn down the risky assignment, but Hemingway was not about to walk away from the chance to write about a critical global event. Firmly, Ernest told his wife that his growth as a writer came first, even before her concern for his safety.

In Constantinople, Hemingway absorbed the misery of a countryside torn by war, translating it into brilliant, moving dispatches. The lead sentence of his first article from the war zone showed his new skill at using a handful of words to express a complex situation: "Constantinople is noisy, hot, hilly, dirty, and beautiful . . . packed with uniforms and rumors."[22]

In the aftermath of World War I, western Turkey forced its Greek residents out of Anatolia and neighboring provinces. Hemingway recorded their grim exodus from their homes:

> In a never-ending staggering march the Christian population of Eastern Thrace is jamming the roads toward Macedonia. . . . They don't know where they are going. They left their farms, villages and ripe, brown fields and joined the main stream of refugees when they heard the Turk was coming. Now they can only keep their places in the ghastly procession while the mudsplashed Greek cavalry herd them along like cow-punchers driving steers.[23]

Joining the Club

As he developed a personal voice in both his fiction writing and his *Star* articles, Hemingway's ambition to join the Left Bank's trendy group of artists and writers became a reality. The letters of introduction Sherwood Anderson had written for him opened the door to a meeting with Ezra Pound, a wild-haired experimental poet who was one of the editors of an important magazine, *The Little Review.*

Pound had strong opinions on literature and was happy to offer his advice to the talented would-be novelist. Hemingway was equally eager to learn all he could from

One of the many American artists Hemingway met in Paris was poet Ezra Pound. Pound's writing and advice had a profound influence on Hemingway.

Pound. At the poet's home, Hemingway respectfully took in Pound's intense speeches on writing. "He listened at Pound's feet as to an oracle," Hadley said later. "I believe some of the ideas lasted all his life." [24] Like Grace Hall Hemingway, Ezra Pound believed artists should work hard, perfecting their craft as faithfully as a pianist practices music. He also believed in using a lean writing style, free of unnecessary words, an approach Hemingway was already trying out.

Hemingway was thrilled that the respected poet thought highly enough of his work to give him advice on his literary career. But it hurt his pride a little to have to ask for help. In a display of immaturity, Hemingway wrote a sketch making fun of Pound, whose self-important manner and untrimmed beard made him an easy target to mock. He toyed with the disastrous idea of submitting the satire to Pound's magazine. Fortunately for Hemingway's future, the young man thought better of insulting his mentor. Instead, they became friends. Hemingway bragged, "He's teaching me to write, and I'm teaching him to box." [25] Pound recommended Hemingway's work to several editors.

Gertrude Stein's Support

In the spring of 1922, the Hemingways had visited another important friend of Sherwood Anderson's, the writer Gertrude Stein. In her work, Stein's use of language was so experimental it was often hard even for sophisticated readers, let alone scholars, to understand. Even so, by the time she met Hemingway in her forties, Gertrude Stein had already made a name for herself as a unique voice in literature. Stein was a large, confident woman who cut her hair like a man's. She threw popular parties for Europe's new and established artists and writers. Her home was filled with works by modern painters who are world famous today—Cézanne, Matisse, Picasso.

Hemingway joined the elite group and soon became one of Stein's favorite people. In turn, he was fascinated by her. She did not seem to care what people thought of her, and she always spoke her mind. He asked her to read his fiction, including a novel fragment. At the Hemingways' small flat, Stein settled herself on the bed in the living room and read through it all. Although Stein praised most of Hemingway's work, she suggested that he tone down his overly detailed descriptions. And she gave blunt advice: "Begin over again and concentrate."[26] Hemingway was not insulted. He thought she was right.

Pressure to Produce

Unfortunately, the young writer on the brink of his career soon had to begin over again in a way he had not expected. In the fall of 1922, Hemingway went to Switzerland on assignment for the *Star*. He invited Hadley to join him there for a ski vacation. As a surprise, she packed all his manuscripts into a suitcase, in case he wanted to work on his fiction while vacationing. On the train, the suitcase disappeared, apparently stolen. Hadley sobbed all the way to Switzerland. Remembering how upset Hadley was when she broke the news of the theft to him, her husband later wrote: "I had never seen anyone hurt by a thing other than death or unbearable suffering, except Hadley when she told me about the

Another of Hemingway's mentors from his days in Paris was Gertrude Stein. Though she admired most of his work, she advised him to tone down his descriptive passages.

things being gone."[27] Hemingway tried not to panic, hoping that the carbon copies were still back home in Paris. But Hadley had packed the copies in the suitcase, too.

Except for two short stories, Hemingway lost everything he had labored over for so long. He was exhausted by the mere thought of re-creating it all. He had driven himself to produce something worthwhile, and losing what he had created was a crushing defeat. For the first time since his arrival in Paris, Hemingway could not write. Trying to regain his enthusiasm, he joined Hadley and Ezra Pound at Rapallo, an Italian resort, for hiking and skiing. But in Rapallo, Hemingway still could not write, even though his work was the most important activity in his life. Despairing, he wondered if he would ever write again.

But before the couple left the resort, they met a man whose encouragement recharged Hemingway's confidence. At Ernest's request, Edward O'Brien, a poet who was editing a short story collection, read one of Hemingway's stories that had escaped the suitcase. "My Old Man" was about a boy who discovers his jockey father is a crook. The story impressed O'Brien. He offered to include it in his upcoming anthology, *The Best Short Stories of 1923*. The anthology was for previously published stories. "My Old Man" was unpublished. But O'Brien liked Hemingway's story so much, he was willing to waive the rules.

That victory was a turning point. Hemingway cared about what respected writers and editors thought of his work. O'Brien's opinion that "My Old Man" was worth publishing caused Hemingway to take heart at a point when his self-confidence was faltering. Maybe, as Stein had suggested, he really could begin again. When the Hemingways moved on from Rapallo to Cortina, another ski resort, Ernest felt inspiration percolating. He wrote "Out of Season," his first story to use an approach that Hemingway later became known for.

Finding a Voice

"Out of Season" was Hemingway's first experiment with what he later called his "iceberg" method. The story of a young couple and a seedy villager was actually about a suicide, but the suicide was never mentioned. This unspoken event was the hidden foundation below the surface story, like the huge percentage of an iceberg that lurks underwater, invisible. Hemingway later explained, "I had omitted the real end of [the story] which was that the old man hanged himself . . . you could omit anything if you knew that you omitted and the omitted part would strengthen the story and make people feel something more than they understood."[28] The shocking event that is never described was actually the heart of the story. Hemingway hoped to guide his readers, with simple storytelling, to the understanding of a deeper truth than met the eye.

Still in his twenties, Hemingway was on his way to becoming a respected talent. Writing remained his first priority. Even fatherhood did not distract him from his work. In 1923, their son John was born in Toronto, where the couple had temporarily relocated in order to make applying for the baby's American citizenship easier. In Canada, Hemingway worked briefly at the Star offices for an editor he did not get along with. His heart was no longer in journalism. He quit his job, and within months the young family was back in Paris. When he wasn't pushing "Bumby" in his stroller, Hemingway concentrated on writing a series of interconnected stories about a young man named Nick Adams.

Hemingway used Nick to talk about things that loomed large in his own life, past and present—family problems, lost love, patriotism, marriage. Ernest created the character in his own image. Nick was a doctor's son. He had been wounded in World War I. And like Ernest, Nick was struggling to heal his wounds, both physical and emotional, after the horror of battle was over.

In seven months, Hemingway wrote nine stories, many of them tracking Nick Adams's growth from innocence to manhood. In "Indian Camp," a young Nick witnesses a birth and a death in one night. In

"Big Two-Hearted River," about an older Nick Adams, Hemingway again built the story's action above an "iceberg" of submerged emotion. This time the buried part of the iceberg is the war. According to editor Charles Poore in *The Hemingway Reader:* "'Big Two-Hearted River' is a story about a boy who has come back from the war. The war is never mentioned. That is one of the things that gives it the undertones and overtones of a timeless experience." [29] "Big Two-Hearted River" goes beyond describing a particular war in a particular time period. Instead, through Hemingway's subtle handling, it becomes a story about the consequences of any war, in any time period.

Hemingway's new approach to universal themes like love and war attracted an increasing number of readers. "Indian Camp" appeared in the *Transatlantic Review.* His first book, *Three Stories and Ten Poems,* was published in 1923 by a small Parisian press, and followed in 1924 by the acclaimed *In Our Time,* a book of short stories and vignettes. Soon after *In Our Time* appeared, a major American publishing house, Boni and Liveright, offered Hemingway a contract. Hemingway signed happily. He was finally winning the recognition he had worked for.

Rivalry

Hemingway was not the only young American writer making a success of himself in Paris. F. Scott Fitzgerald, also in his twenties, was already the author of the bestseller *This Side of Paradise* and the groundbreaking *The Great Gatsby* when Hemingway met him in a Paris nightclub called the Dingo Bar in 1925. Hemingway thought Scott was an excellent writer. He appreciated his talent, but he was determined to compete with Scott for the world's attention. Feeling superior to his new rival was easy for Hemingway, since Scott had not served overseas in the

Almost Holy

In August 1924, Hemingway composed a passage for inclusion in "Big Two-Hearted River" that showed, through his character Nick Adams, part of the author's developing views on life and art. He later deleted it from the story. The excerpt is reprinted in Carlos Baker's Ernest Hemingway: A Life Story.

"[Nick] wanted to be a great writer. He was pretty sure he would be. . . . It was hard to be a great writer if you loved the world and living in it and special people. It was hard when you loved so many places. . . . He, Nick, wanted to write about country so it would be there like Cézanne had done it in painting. You had to do it from inside yourself. . . . He felt almost holy about it. It was deadly serious. You could do it if you would fight it out. If you'd lived right with your eyes. It was a thing you couldn't talk about."

war, and he passed out whenever he drank liquor (which he did often). The macho, hard-drinking Hemingway found these facts pathetic.

Fitzgerald had already read *In Our Time* before he ever met Hemingway. He told his own editor, Maxwell Perkins of Scribner's, that he thought Hemingway was "the real thing." Scott's generous nature soon won Hemingway's trust. And his brilliance won Hemingway's respect. After reading Fitzgerald's *The Great Gatsby,* Hemingway pledged: "When I had finished the book I knew that no matter what Scott did, nor how he behaved, I must know it was like a sickness and be of any help I could to him and try to be a good friend."[30] The behavior Ernest pledged to overlook was Scott's alcoholism, which caused him to behave strangely. But in years to come, Hemingway's friendship with his fellow writer would be strained.

While his ego demanded unconditional loyalty from his talented friends, Hemingway often put them down. This unkind tendency stands out in his treatment of Sherwood Anderson, the author whose warm letters of introduction had helped Ernest hook up with the Paris literary scene. In 1925, Boni and Liveright published a new Anderson novel, *Dark Laughter.* Hemingway did not like the book, judging it as a comedown from Anderson's earlier works. He was also annoyed that reviewers saw similarities between his own work and Anderson's. Hemingway wanted to be seen as an individual, not a clone of another author. While at work on what would become his first great novel, Hemingway wrote a satire ridiculing *Dark Laughter.* He called it *The Torrents of Spring.*

Hemingway figured that his current publisher, Boni and Liveright, would not publish a cruel send-up of one of their own authors. That was fine with Ernest. He had been trying to think of a way to get out of his original three-book commitment to the publisher so he could sign up with his friend Fitzgerald's editor at Scribner's. Max Perkins had expressed interest in this powerful new talent Fitzgerald was calling "the real thing." Hemingway offered *The Torrents of Spring* to Boni and Liveright, who rejected it. This released Hemingway from his contract and allowed him to sign up with Scribner's.

F. Scott Fitzgerald, author of The Great Gatsby, *met Hemingway in a Paris nightclub. The two writers admired each other's work and became friends, but Hemingway saw Fitzgerald as a rival as well.*

Tough Guy

Publisher Robert McAlmon had mixed feelings about Hemingway when he first met him but later published Hemingway's first book. McAlmon's description of Hemingway is from Carlos Baker's Ernest Hemingway: A Life Story.

"At times [Hemingway] was deliberately hard-boiled and case-hardened. Again he appeared deliberately innocent, sentimental, the hurt, soft, but fairly sensitive boy trying to conceal hurt, wanting to be brave, not bitter or cynical but being somewhat both, and somehow on the defensive, suspicions lurking in his peering analytic glances at a person with whom he was talking. He approached a café with a small-boy tough-guy swagger, and before strangers of whom he was doubtful, a potential snarl of scorn played on his large-lipped rather loose mouth."

That was not the end of the humiliation for Anderson, however. Although Hemingway's wife and friends tried to point out that it was uncharitable to seek another publisher for *Torrents,* the author offered it to Scribner's. The silly parody was published in May 1926. Most reviewers got a kick out of it, but Anderson was offended and embarrassed. Hemingway later regretted his shabby treatment of his former friend:

> You shouldn't give it to another writer, I mean really give it to him. I know you shouldn't do it because I did it once to Sherwood Anderson. I did it because I was righteous, which is the worst thing you can be, and I thought he was going to pot by the way he was writing, and I could kid him out of it by showing him how awful it was . . . the only thing I can say is that I was as cruel to myself then.[31]

The Sun Also Rises

Torrents was his first published novel, but Hemingway had already completed the first draft, back in the fall of 1925, of a book that would make a name for him as a serious writer. He spent months revising the manuscript he had originally completed in several weeks. Finally, in October 1926, Scribner's published *The Sun Also Rises*. Originally titled *Fiesta,* the novel explored the empty, irresponsible behavior of a group of young men and women mingling at a bullfight fiesta in Pamplona, Spain. Their dreams have been shattered by the horror of World War I. For this reason, Hemingway had considered calling the novel "The Lost Generation." *The Sun Also Rises* was a hit, racing through three printings and winning rave reviews for its vivid dialogue, tense action, and emotionally detached cast of characters.

Where did Hemingway get the inspiration for his first great novel? He had witnessed his first bullfight in Pamplona in 1923, while vacationing with Hadley shortly before Bumby's birth. Gertrude Stein had planted the seeds for the author's growing obsession with the bloody activity, by sharing her views on the bullfight as ritual. The brutal ceremony of the bullfight reminded Hemingway of a stage play about the certainty of death. Hemingway spilled out his fascination with the bullring in a *Star* article that spring:

[The bullfighter's face] glistened with sweat in the sun but was almost expressionless . . . he was studying the bull because a few minutes later it would be his duty to kill him, and once he went out with his thin, red-hilted sword and his piece of red cloth to kill the bull in the final set it would be him or the bull.[32]

The idea of the bullfighter rebelling against death, killing before he himself is killed, was one Hemingway would return to many times in his life's work.

Romero's Purity of Line

At the festival in Pamplona in Hemingway's The Sun Also Rises, *Jake Barnes, a writer, explains to his friend Lady Brett Ashley why Romero's bullfighting technique is admirable. Hemingway admired matadors because they faced death bravely. He believed that the challenges a writer faces are similar to those faced by the bullfighter. This excerpt is taken from* The Hemingway Reader, *edited by Charles Poore.*

"Romero never made any contortions, always it was straight and pure and natural in line. The others twisted themselves like corkscrews, their elbows raised, and leaned against the flanks of the bull after his horns had passed, to give a faked look of danger. Afterward, all that was faked turned bad and gave an unpleasant feeling. Romero's bull-fighting gave real emotion, because he kept the absolute purity of line in his movements and always quietly and calmly let the horns pass him close each time. He did not have to emphasize their closeness. Brett saw how something that was beautiful done close to the bull was ridiculous if it were done a little way off. I told her how since the death of Joselito all the bull-fighters had been developing a technic that simulated this appearance of danger in order to give a fake emotional feeling, while the bull-fighter was really safe. Romero had the old thing, the holding of his purity of line through the maximum of exposure, while he dominated the bull by making him realize he was unattainable, while he prepared him for the killing.

'I've never seen him do an awkward thing,' Brett said.
'You won't until he gets frightened,' I said."

The bloody spectacle of bullfighting was one of the influences for Hemingway's first masterpiece, The Sun Also Rises.

The Sun Also Rises flowed from other sources as well. His new novel's themes of lost hope and the possibility for hope's renewal came from a more intimate part of Ernest's life—his past pain. He had known the merciless brutality of the battlefield, its violence lacking even the measured dignity of the bullring. And he had lost his innocent belief in romantic love with the downfall of his relationship with Agnes. These personal setbacks had plunged him into depression. He had emerged cockier, tougher.

His new attitude made him a little like the main character of *The Sun Also Rises*, Jake Barnes. Barnes is a journalist whose World War I wounds, both physical and emotional, don't show. Instead Barnes, like his equally tough girlfriend Lady Brett Ashley, covers his scars with a whitewash of cool. In a famous exchange at the end of the novel, Brett tells Jake they could have had "such a damned good time together." Masking his mixed emotions with a clever line, Jake says, "Isn't it pretty to think so?"[33] The characters in *The Sun Also Rises* ask for little more out of life than good times. To Hemingway, that's part of their tragedy. But Hemingway's title, a quote from Ecclesiastes, hints to readers that hope circles back around as regularly as the sun rises each morning.

Not all readers caught the hopeful glint in the dark novel. Despite their pride in his achievement, Hemingway's parents were shocked by the characters' drunkenness and immorality and did not hesitate to tell him so. But Hemingway had other family matters on his mind.

Pauline Pfeiffer, an American editor for the Paris *Vogue*, had befriended Ernest and Hadley and spent many vacations with them, growing extremely close to the couple. The petite, brunette woman fell in love with Hemingway. Instead of respecting the Hemingways' marriage commitment, Pauline grabbed every chance she could to get Ernest to notice her.

Ernest was not an innocent bystander in the seduction. He was attracted to Pauline.

In addition to being intelligent, Pauline was extremely rich—her uncle owned a cosmetics empire. Hemingway was flattered by Pfeiffer's attentiveness and excited by the idea of more than one woman being in love with him. When Hadley learned of his involvement with Pauline, she was heartsick. But she hoped that if Ernest and Pauline agreed to spend one hundred days apart, their mutual infatuation would wither. Hadley and Ernest took separate residences. Pauline Pfeiffer sailed for New York. Hemingway was torn. He missed Hadley and still loved her, but he also longed for Pauline. His guilt and confusion over these feelings plunged him into another depression.

In a letter to Scott Fitzgerald, Hemingway wrote that his good life with Hadley

Hemingway's marriage to Hadley fell apart in Paris. Ernest met another woman, an American editor named Pauline Pfeiffer (far right). Despite feeling immense guilt about it, he left Hadley for Pauline in 1927.

had become hell on earth when he met Pauline, and that his marriage's collapse was all his own fault. Although he tried to make a joke of the matter, he also admitted to Scott that for many months he had been struggling to get to sleep and spent hours each night brooding over his problems. Hemingway's troubled nights were signs that depression had returned.

Ernest also confided his worries to Pauline Pfeiffer, writing that he was considering killing himself to cancel out the harm he felt he'd done. At least if he died, he said, then Hadley would not end up a divorced woman. And Pauline would not be a home-wrecker. When Pauline wrote back to him and assured him that she was still committed to being with him, he cheered up a little. But he still could not shake the blues. Regularly, each evening around 5 P.M., he found himself tangled in feelings of hopelessness, fear, and self-blame. These stubborn black moods sapped his enthusiasm for his writing projects. Ernest could see only one honorable way out of the snare he had fallen into—

ending his marriage to Hadley. But he could not bring himself to make the break official.

Hadley could see from her husband's anguish that the one-hundred-day separation agreement would not result in a reconciliation after all. She canceled it and asked Ernest to follow through with a legal divorce instead, so that she and Bumby could get on with their lives. The Hemingways divorced, and Ernest married Pauline Pfeiffer in 1927. Thanks to his new wife, Hemingway was now a wealthy man, free to write at leisure. In 1928, after Pauline became pregnant with their first child, they moved to Key West, Florida. The author saw his young son Bumby at regular intervals.

Before the age of thirty, Hemingway had shown the world he was a talent worth watching. Single-minded commitment to his craft and determined networking had allowed him to achieve his goal. His focus on his own achievements had cost him a marriage. But he still had his work ahead of him.

3 Defending Champion

Ernest Hemingway started his writing career as an unknown in Paris. Suddenly, *The Sun Also Rises* rocketed him to stardom. In the beginning, he wrote fiction without a strong voice of his own. In *The Sun Also Rises,* he found one that was both tough and tender. Back in the United States, Hemingway no longer had to sell editors on his talent. Instead, the world waited eagerly for his next book. His sudden success, however, did not bring him peace of mind. Instead, like a prizefighter defending his title, Hemingway could not forget that a false move, a momentary weakness on his part, could bring him to his knees in front of his audience. And that was a humiliation he was determined to avoid. Unfortunately, over the next decade, the pressures of fame and the stress of constantly pushing for excellence in his work would often tempt him to act foolishly.

A Father's Suicide

In late 1928, a sad event shook Hemingway's self-confidence. At the same time, it strengthened his desire to prove himself to the world. While Hemingway was on vacation with Bumby, a telegram brought the author the shocking news of his father's death. He rushed to his old family home in Oak Park, where he was stunned to hear that his father had deliberately shot himself. Ed had looked sad and ill when Ernest had seen him earlier that year, but his son had never suspected anything like this would happen. The rest of the family filled him in.

Ed's attitude and health had both been slipping for a long time. He had been suffering from chest pains, but he refused to get treatment for his heart condition, even though he was a physician himself. He had also discovered that he was diabetic. That meant he would need to follow a strict low-sugar diet. But the man who was always active was frantic over the prospect of a serious illness controlling his life and slowing him down.

In addition to health problems, Hemingway's father was running from financial worries. Ed and Grace had invested in Florida real estate, expecting it to go up in value and help support them in their old age. But the payments on the Florida lots drained the family finances. Afraid of losing his investment, Ed asked his brother, Ernest's Uncle George, for a loan to cover the payments. Instead, George urged Ed to sell the land. But Ed could not admit defeat, preferring to cling to an investment he could no longer afford to pay for. Distressed about his health and worried about his family's financial future, Ed delayed making the decision to sell. Meanwhile, his debts piled higher.

According to his daughter Marcelline, Ed had been withdrawing from the family during this difficult time, "almost as though he defied anyone to get close to him, or understand or help him."[34] Showing more signs of depression, Ernest's father also became irritable and suspicious, snapping at his family and spending time behind locked doors. He seemed afraid to be alone, but equally unable to discuss his worries with Grace or the rest of the family. The only person he seemed to want near him was his younger son, Les.

Enmeshed in mounting confusion, Ed woke on the morning of December 6 with

In late 1928 Hemingway's father, after a long bout with depression and failing health, committed suicide in the family home in Oak Park.

a stabbing pain in his foot. He suspected gangrene, a decaying of tissues from lack of blood supply, often caused by untreated diabetes. If Ed did have gangrene, he knew that his leg might have to be amputated. He promised Grace he would have the pain checked out after his morning hospital rounds. But instead, Ed returned home at noon, told Grace he was going to take a nap, climbed the stairs to his room, and shot himself in the head. Les, home in bed with a cold, heard the gun go off, once. He never forgot the sound.

A Son's Grief

After the funeral, Hemingway joined forces with the rest of his family, trying to make sense of the tragedy. While sifting through the jumble of financial papers Ed had let pile up during his long depression, Hemingway repeatedly asked himself whether or not there was something he could have done to prevent his father's suicide. If only Ed had asked him for money, he and Pauline could have lent him some, Ernest would think. Then he reminded himself that his father had been too sick to think clearly. No amount of money would have been enough.

From Oak Park, Hemingway scribbled a sad note to Scott about his father's death: "My father shot himself as I suppose you may have read in the papers. . . . I was fond as hell of my father and feel too . . . sick . . . to write a letter."[35] Hemingway had always felt a bond with his powerful, vibrant father. And Ed had been proud of his son's career, even when he and Grace questioned the morality of what Ernest wrote about—and they had questioned it often.

Hemingway (pictured here with his parents and Pauline) blamed his mother, Grace—with whom he already had a strained relationship—for his father's lapse into the depression that led to his suicide.

But Ed had couched his criticism in love. After reading *In Our Time,* he had written this gentle suggestion to his son: "Trust you will see and describe more of humanity of a different character in future volumes. . . . The brutal you have surely shown the world. Look for the joyous, uplifting, and optimistic and spiritual in character. It is present if found."[36] Hemingway's father believed in focusing on the positive in life. Ironically, Ed's overpowering depression kept him from remembering his own advice.

In the end, his son had to grieve for him under the world's unblinking gaze. Even though his father had lost his battle with depression, Hemingway aimed to keep taking on life's challenges without choking. Sadly, one way Ernest coped with the shock of his father's suicide was to blame his own mother for it. After all, he reasoned, Grace had insisted on buying a vacation cottage for her private use as a retreat. Ed had bitterly objected to the extra expense, but Grace, who usually got her way, persuaded him to give in. Maybe Ed's money troubles were her fault, her son thought. And, Hemingway recalled, Grace could be cold and judgmental—he'd been on the receiving end of her disapproval plenty of times himself. Hemingway wondered whether his mother had let his father down when he needed her most.

Blaming Grace

Ernest's feelings about this strong, opinionated woman who was so like himself were already shaky. In his hurt and anger over losing his father, Grace was an easy target to blame. Although he and Pauline eventually arranged for a trust fund for Grace that helped support her financially for the rest of her life, Ernest was never close to his mother again. He often spoke bitterly about her to friends and rarely phoned, wrote, or visited her although she kept in touch with him regularly.

After her husband's death, Grace Hall Hemingway stayed independent and active. She continued teaching music, learned to drive, and took up landscape painting. Like her son, she was a fighter. As biographer Bernice Kert points out, the very qualities that caused mother and son to clash were the ones that kept them going in bad times: "the stubborn belief in [their] own opinions, the self-importance, the pride and vanity."[37] These rather negative traits helped them to think highly of themselves and shrug off self-doubt.

Why would Hemingway blame his mother for Ed's suicide, something neither he nor she could control? Partly because his father's mood swings reminded Hemingway of his own. According to author Michael Reynolds: "He wants to blame the father's death on the mother . . . because that is easier than admitting his father's 'nervousness' is like his own, highs and lows cycling each time a little farther down that dark road."[38] It was easier for Ernest to blame Grace than to face the possibility that severe depression ran in the family. Hating his mother distracted Hemingway from his fear of losing control of his own hard-won reputation—and perhaps even his sanity.

As it had during many other hard times, Hemingway's writing helped him survive the pain of his father's suicide.

Hard work counterbalanced his fears that somewhere inside himself lurked the same weakness that killed his father. Shaping the manuscript that would soon become his next published novel also reassured him that he would continue to produce books that touched readers, won him praise, and kept his reputation alive. As long as he could write, he could feel powerful and in control, keep depression at bay—and survive to keep on writing.

A Farewell to Arms

A few months after his father's death, Hemingway finished the novel he had been working on since the previous spring. *A Farewell to Arms* ("arms" meaning weapons) was a World War I novel that drew from all his memories of the sights and sounds of war-torn Italy. Since Hemingway had seen less than a month of combat, however, he did not have many firsthand memories to draw on for battle scenes. That did not stop him from inventing scenes that pulled readers into the thick of the narrative. According to Reynolds: "From maps, books, and close listening, he . . . made up a war he never saw, described terrain he never walked, and re-created the retreat from Caporetto so accurately that his Italian readers will later say he was present."[39] Hemingway's continued practice of watching and listening to people helped him re-create shared human experiences in his books in a way readers found exciting and believable.

By contrast, for the romantic part of the story, Hemingway called upon intimate personal experience. He did not have to improvise the emotions and physical images of his friendship with Agnes von Kurowsky, the former girlfriend who had broken up with him nearly a decade earlier. He clearly remembered both the relationship and its seismic impact on him. For *A Farewell to Arms,* Hemingway uses Agnes as the model

Masked Emotion

In a discussion of A Farewell to Arms, *originally published in 1965 and reprinted in* Readings on Ernest Hemingway, *Carlos Baker discusses the strong emotion apparent in Hemingway's next-to-last version of the ending of the book. That intense emotion is "masked" in the final version that appears in the published novel. According to Baker, the earlier version reveals that Hemingway was capable of great emotion, which he often hid from others.*

"[In] the famous conclusion [to *A Farewell to Arms,*] . . . Catherine dies and her lover says a silent farewell before he walks back to the hotel alone in the falling rain. . . . Hemingway spent considerable effort on the conclusion, and . . . the final version, familiar to readers since 1929, is almost infinitely superior to the [next-to-last] version, which has only recently come to light. . . .

The [next-to-last] version is another matter entirely, and it is very revealing. In place of the laconic interchange between Henry and the attending surgeon, the visit to the room to say goodbye, and the lonely walk back to the hotel in the rain, we have three quite different paragraphs. . . . All the sharp poignancy of the final version is here blunted and destroyed. What is worse, the words themselves seem moist with self-pity. . . .

The rather [talkative] self-pity, . . . when we [compare] it with . . . the final version, . . . suggests . . . that the stoicism of the last version was only a mask, adopted and assumed for dramatic show, while under it Hemingway's still wounded feelings were bleeding . . . almost as intensively as they had been doing ten years before. Within the short space of seven months, he had been badly smashed up in both war and love. Now, much later, his double wound of body and soul rose to the surface of his memory. . . .

The stoic mask, assumed as a façade to conceal the psychic warfare which is going on beneath, may help us to explain and to understand much of the braggadocio [boasting] which struck his detractors as all too apparent in Hemingway's later life. It may also explain his [taking on] the stoic code as a standard of behavior—a standard to which he required all his later heroes to conform."

for the character of Catherine, a beautiful English army nurse in love with a wounded American ambulance driver.

A Farewell to Arms, though, is more than just a love story. It quickly won acclaim as one of the most realistic and probing war novels of all time. Hemingway's young couple try to walk away from war's madness. But they run up against sorrow, instead. The novel showed that Hemingway believed that evil was always in ambush, and that the best people, who tried hardest to live honorably, often seemed to be the hardest hit by its potshots. He included these lines in the novel:

> The world breaks everyone and afterward many are strong at the broken places. But those that will not break it kills. It kills the very good and the very gentle and the very brave impartially. If you are none of these you can be sure it will kill you, too, but there will be no special hurry.[40]

Hemingway believed that people who were blessed in some way usually suffered most in life. The author himself had already weathered much pain, both in World War I and in his personal life, most recently with the loss of his father. Now he was "strong at the broken places." And he was determined to keep his resistance up.

Another Success

It was common for a publisher to release selections from upcoming books for publication in a popular magazine as previews to arouse reader interest. Before publication as a book, installments of *A Farewell to Arms* came out in *Scribner's Magazine.* The $16,000 payment Hemingway received in January 1929 for the magazine sale was the largest amount *Scribner's* had ever paid any author. In the fall of 1929, after its magazine release, the book was shipped to bookstores, around the same time as another great war novel, Erich Maria Remarque's *All Quiet on the Western Front.*

Reviewers and readers loved *A Farewell to Arms.* The author's reputation was secure—for the time being. And thanks to the extra income from the new novel, plus the constant of Pauline's money, the Hemingways stayed wealthy during the huge U.S. stock market crash of October 1929 that triggered the Great Depression.

The couple took advantage of their good fortune during the country's Depression years. They went marlin fishing in Cuba, bullfight hopping in Spain, and big-game hunting in Africa. In Paris, they visited old friends. Always ready for a little friendly competition, Hemingway challenged the men to boxing matches. His choice of aggressive, traditionally masculine activities was deliberate. He knew the world was watching. He had a tough, rebellious image to keep up, and he lived the part, as if to reassure himself that life could not bring him down, whatever it threw at him.

Unfortunately, friends were not always impressed by his act, especially when it went over the edge. During a boxing match with an old friend from Toronto, Morley Callaghan, Hemingway deliberately spit a mouthful of blood in Callaghan's face. Callaghan was insulted, but Ernest did not seem to see why. He explained offhandedly that he was merely repeating a defiant gesture he had seen matadors use in the bullring. Increasingly in Hemingway's personal life, going the distance with style seemed more important than who got trampled along the way.

Rebelling Against Death

Hemingway continued to be a bullfighting fan. He was drawn to the idea of man defying death. Hemingway admired what he saw as the matadors' courage in orchestrating the bull's death, exposing themselves to danger in the process. Because matadors performed their artful cruelty in public, Hemingway believed that they had something in common with writers. According to Reynolds: "While not literally in danger of death while writing, the author lives with the same possibility that his skills will [lessen], that he will fall from the public eye, that his courage will fail."[41]

Hemingway decided his next book would not be a novel, but a mix of facts and his own personal opinions about bullfighting. His obsession with the brutal custom was growing. When visiting Bumby in Paris he met a young American named Sidney Franklin who had become a matador in Spain. Hemingway followed Franklin's career while continuing to work on his bullfight chronicle.

Bullfighting was a fitting subject for an author who felt he was constantly in danger of the "death" of his fame and talent. The stubborn matador confronting the relentless bull was an image Hemingway be-

Hemingway was attracted to bullfighting because he saw the matador's performance as a representation of man's struggle against death.

lieved in, feeling a connection with it. During the writing of what would be titled *Death in the Afternoon,* he wrote his friend Archibald MacLeish (in French): "*Dans la vie, il faut (d'abord) durer.*"[42] This thought—that hanging on, enduring, is the most important thing of all in life—seemed to sum up his admiration for people who fought to survive.

Hemingway also had deeper thoughts about bullfighting's true meaning. He saw matadors not only as survivors, but as men trying to play God. Matadors cannot bring the dead to life. But they can at least feel powerful through their ability to kill, Hemingway observed in his book:

> Once you accept the rule of death thou shalt not kill is an easily, and a naturally obeyed commandment. But when a man is still in rebellion against death he has pleasure in taking to himself one of the Godlike attributes: that of giving it.[43]

Hemingway took an objective stance about why some people, especially matadors, kill. His neutral and knowing tone made many readers of *Death in the Afternoon* wonder if Hemingway actually approved of the violent side of human nature that he commented on.

When *Death in the Afternoon* came out in 1932, Hemingway discovered that many readers did not share his interest in matadors or brutal fights to the death. They thought the whole subject of bullfighting was distasteful and offensive. While the book sold well, partly due to Hemingway's reputation as an important author, many critics found the writer's philosophizing about life and death boring, his obsession with killing unhealthy, and his talk of bravery mere bragging.

A Question of Chest Hair

One review of *Death in the Afternoon,* sarcastically titled "Bull in the Afternoon," enraged Hemingway. Reviewer Max Eastman suggested that Hemingway wrote about the macho sport because he was insecure about his own manhood. Eastman said he found Hemingway's writing phony, like wearing "false hair on the chest."[44] Instead of ignoring Eastman's taunt, Hemingway publicly threatened to sue, which called even more attention to the matter.

Although he did not end up suing Eastman, Hemingway would not drop the quarrel. A few years later, in editor Max Perkins's office, Hemingway unexpectedly ran into Eastman. Hemingway unbuttoned his own shirt to show Eastman his hairy chest. Then he grinned and ripped open Eastman's shirt, exposing the man's hairless chest. To Perkins's relief, both men laughed at Hemingway's exhibition. But the confrontation escalated. Hemingway grabbed a copy of the book containing a reprint of Eastman's original bad review and whacked Eastman in the face with it. Eastman lunged at him. The two grown men rolled on the floor like children, punching each other. The scuffle made the newspapers.

He may have believed he was bravely defending a point of honor. But the incident exposed Hemingway to public criticism. People saw him as immature and self-centered. Even Scott Fitzgerald, whose alcoholism often tempted him to act in equally juvenile ways, was embarrassed for his friend. He wondered if Hemingway was really in charge of his own life to the degree that he boasted. Fitzgerald wrote of the Eastman incident: "[Hemingway] is living at present in a world so entirely his own that it is impossible to help him."[45]

On Safari

The author's obsession with stereotypically macho activities like bullfighting led him to East Africa in 1933. He took his wife along, but left their two young boys, Patrick and Gregory, behind with servants and relatives. For several months, Ernest and Pauline, with the help of a strong, silent guide named Philip Percival, went big-game hunting on the vast Serengeti Plain.

At sunset each evening they returned to camp, their assistants lugging their trophies—carcasses of antelopes, gazelles, leopards, and lions. Hemingway made hunting into a competition, bragging about being the first to shoot a rhinoceros.

Hemingway stopped bragging and sulked when, soon afterward, another hunter shot an even bigger rhino. Hemingway enjoyed himself so much that he foolishly ignored his symptoms when he came down with dysentery. As a result, he developed severe intestinal cramps and had to fly to Nairobi for treatment. But the moment he felt better, he rushed back to his safari adventure.

Back home the following year, the Hemingways invested in an expensive toy, a diesel-powered deep-sea fishing boat for exploring the waters off the Florida coast. Hemingway named the boat the *Pilar,* a Spanish name that was one of his old nicknames for Pauline. Hemingway often carted along a seasick Gregory on his motorings between Key West and Havana—a twenty-six-hour voyage. Many of the marlins Hemingway caught on these fishing trips weighed more than five hundred pounds. Remembering his father's com-

One of Hemingway's trophies from his many African hunting trips decorates the floor in Hemingway House in Havana, Cuba.

Hemingway was an avid deep-sea fisherman. In 1934 Hemingway and his wife bought this boat, which he named the Pilar.

mand not to kill more fish or game than he could eat, the famous author would pose for a photograph with his catch to document his skill. Then he would give the extra fish meat to the hungry Cubans who gathered expectantly around him at the dock.

Although he plunged happily into the sporting life that Pauline financed, Hemingway kept up with his work. His next big project was an autobiographical narrative of his adventures on safari, titled *Green Hills of Africa.* The long, often beautiful account of big-game hunting in the lush African countryside was published in 1935, six years after his last truly successful book, *A Farewell to Arms.* Max Perkins, Hemingway's editor, worried that it would not sell well.

And, in fact, the public did not really know what to make of the book. Was it a novel, a travelogue, or a personal testimony?

Many reviewers loved his descriptions of Africa's pristine landscape and his exciting accounts of actual big-game hunts he'd experienced. But many others wished he would keep his opinionated personal asides on life and literature out of the discussion. In a decision that he later regretted, Hemingway used the pages of *Green Hills of Africa* to speak directly to his past critics, twisting his art into a weapon of self-defense. In one memorable phrase, for example, Hemingway compared a circle of New York writers to worms in a bottle. At another point in the book, he called book critics lice that live off writers.

Hemingway originally had high hopes for *Green Hills of Africa,* feeling that its long scenes maintained their tension and that the sensuous imagery made Africa come alive. He blamed the book's relatively low sales on his publisher and on his critics. To admit that his latest work had failed to match *A Farewell to Arms* in quality or popularity would have been to admit defeat in his continuing battle to stay one step ahead of himself. Hemingway insisted that, in time, the public would come to appreciate the book's greatness.

A Public Confession

In December 1935, Hemingway was disturbed by an article his friend F. Scott Fitzgerald published in *Esquire* magazine called "The Crack-Up." Fitzgerald had been drinking steadily. His wife Zelda was in and out of hospitals with mental illness and Scott was heartbroken at losing her. He felt overwhelmed by his problems. Fitzgerald decided to sell the story of his troubles. He wrote in detail about his sadness and inability to write, admitting that he felt his career was over.

Fitzgerald was being painfully honest about his situation, but Hemingway was shocked by what he saw as a pathetic public statement of failure. Hemingway knew what it was like to feel down. He, too, had experienced many dry spells of gloom and despair, but had found the resources, including his trademark cockiness, to keep struggling forward. And Hemingway, who believed in presenting a strong image to the world, would never have told his public that he felt like giving up. Fitzgerald had done the unthinkable. His friend had

embarrassed himself needlessly, Ernest felt. Hemingway wrote to Max Perkins:

> I always knew he couldn't think—he never could—but he had a marvelous talent and the thing is to use it—not whine in public. Good God, people go through that emptiness many times in life and come out and do work . . . a writer can be a coward but at least he should be a writer . . . but it's so damned easy to criticize our friends and I shouldn't write this. I wish we could help him.[46]

Fitzgerald's embarrassing article reminded Hemingway of his own continual fear of losing his touch as a writer. His letter to Perkins seemed almost a pep talk to himself.

In fact, in January 1936, only a month after reading Fitzgerald's depressing article, Hemingway suffered through a three-week episode of sleeplessness and deep sadness himself. By now, these episodes of depression had become routine. The author pulled himself out of this one by forcing himself to get out and exercise and telling himself to try to worry less about how well and how fast he was writing. Soon, he was back at work, creating a series of stories inspired by his African safaris.

"The Snows of Kilimanjaro"

Many of the safari stories—such as "The Short Happy Life of Francis Macomber," which appeared in *Cosmopolitan* magazine and told of a beautiful rich woman who shoots her husband instead of a charging buffalo—were hailed as excellent. They remain some of the author's most popular

"Get in Somebody Else's Head"

In a fictionalized article for Esquire in 1935 in which he calls himself Y.C. for "Your Correspondent," Hemingway offers advice to a young would-be writer nicknamed "Mice," short for "Maestro," who tags along with him on a fishing trip from Key West to Cuba. This excerpt is taken from "Monologue to the Maestro: A High Seas Letter," collected in By-Line: Ernest Hemingway, edited by William White.

"MICE: How can a writer train himself?

Y.C.: Watch what happens today. If we get into a fish see exactly what it is that everyone does. If you get a kick out of it while he is jumping remember back until you see exactly what the action was that gave you the emotion. Whether it was the rising of the line from the water and the way it tightened like a fiddle string until drops started from it, or the way he smashed and threw water when he jumped. Remember what the noises were and what was said. Find what gave you the emotion; what the action was that gave you the excitement. Then write it down making it clear so the reader will see it too and have the same feeling that you had. . . .

MICE: All right.

Y.C.: Then get in somebody else's head for a change. If I bawl you out try to figure what I'm thinking about as well as how you feel about it. If Carlos curses Juan think what both their sides of it are. Don't just think who is right. . . . As a man you know who is right and who is wrong. . . . As a writer you should not judge. You should understand.

MICE: All right.

Y.C.: Listen now. When people talk listen completely. Don't be thinking what you're going to say. Most people never listen. Nor do they observe. You should be able to go into a room and when you come out know everything that you saw there and not only that. If that room gave you any feeling you should know exactly what it was that gave you that feeling. Try that for practice. When you're in town stand outside the theatre and see how the people differ in the way they get out of taxis or motor cars. There are a thousand ways to practice. And always think of other people."

works today. The best of them, "The Snows of Kilimanjaro," was Hemingway's way of translating into art his fear of failing to live up to the promise of his own great talent. In this story, a writer lies dying in Africa, waiting with his rich wife for a rescue plane that arrives too late. Significantly, the writer is dying of gangrene, the disease that sparked the suicide of Hemingway's father. The nature of the disease suggests that the writer is "rotting" away, the purity of his talent corrupted by his need for fame and fortune.

While the story is filled with fragments of Hemingway's personal life, the towering image of Mount Kilimanjaro dominates the story. Many readers see the huge mountain as a symbol of the dizzying height Hemingway himself had resolved to climb in his literary career. As writer Richard O'Connor puts it: "Hemingway worried that his own career was still on the lower slopes of Kilimanjaro and that something—perhaps death, perhaps the decay of his talent—would prevent him from climbing higher and higher toward the peak of achievement he believed himself capable of reaching."[47]

A Cracked Friendship

When Scott Fitzgerald opened his copy of the August 1936 issue of *Esquire* containing "The Snows of Kilimanjaro," he was stunned and angered to see his own name mentioned in the story. Hemingway's dying writer remembers a man he once knew, "poor Scott Fitzgerald," a fool who had been "wrecked" by his worship of rich people. Hemingway's attack on Fitzgerald seemed calculated to show the public that Hemingway did not consider himself anything like Fitzgerald. By accusing Scott of weakness, Ernest distracted himself and his audience from his fears that his own talent and reputation might not last.

Fitzgerald demanded that Hemingway "lay off" him in print. Furthermore, he asked that Hemingway remove the Fitzgerald reference when the story was published in book form. That request was eventually granted—Fitzgerald's name was changed. But in the meantime, Hemingway responded that he could write about anyone he pleased and say whatever he wanted. He told Max Perkins that he was surprised Scott had anything to say in his own defense after publishing "awful things" about himself in "The Crack-Up."

Floored by Hemingway's rude, irresponsible attitude, Fitzgerald decided to keep his distance from his friend. Having problems of his own, it was easy for Scott to see that Hemingway was troubled. In fact, Scott wondered if Ernest had gone insane. Scott believed that Ernest's problem was an irrational belief in his own greatness. What Fitzgerald did not see, because Hemingway was determined to hide the truth, was that the macho author's episodes of "playing God" were only the tip of the iceberg. Lying beneath the surface was the secret of Hemingway's continual self-doubt, his nagging fear that he would never live to reach his personal mountaintop.

New Battles

Instead of taking a calm look at his problems, Hemingway drove himself into frantic activity, both in his work and in his personal life. In 1937, he published *To Have and*

Have Not, about a cocky smuggler named Harry Morgan who resembled the author's idea of himself as a brash hero. While it was not a masterpiece, Hemingway gained confidence after writing it, because for the first time he tried writing in the third person, using "he" rather than "I," as if watching the action rather than living it. The successful experiment with a new approach strengthened his faith in his ability to grow as a writer.

Meanwhile Hemingway had made the acquaintance of an attractive and intelligent writer, Martha Gellhorn, whose work had been favorably compared to his own. Twenty-seven years of age to his thirty-six, "Marty" was a big fan of his books. In 1936, traveling to Key West with her mother, she happened to meet Hemingway and they struck up a friendship. Ernest's guilt and embarrassment about living mainly on his wife's money had already weakened his marriage to Pauline when Martha entered his life. In addition, Pauline's constant demands on his attention had started to bore him. This new woman had a career and lively ideas of her own. And her interest in him pumped him with renewed confidence in his manhood.

As the globe began rumbling with the unrest that would soon explode into World War II, Hemingway was looking for new battles to fight. In the next few years he would shake off his alliance to Pauline Pfeiffer in favor of a brief, stormy marriage to Marty Gellhorn. Both writers would become embroiled in the war effort. In fact, the war became the next battlefield for Hemingway's violent struggles with his life and his art.

Chapter

4 Self-Absorption

For Ernest Hemingway, the years that included World War II were a time of self-absorption. Always walking carefully to keep from stumbling into another depression, struggling to maintain his reputation as a renowned author, and fretting about getting older, Hemingway wanted to feel young, brilliant, and strong. To that end, he continued to act the part of a macho man. He also began drinking too much, and that piled extra strain on his physical and mental health. His narrow focus on his own needs and his lack of consideration for people close to him damaged his relationships. These personal troubles in turn disrupted the writing projects he was concerned about completing. Thanks to Ernest Hemingway's strong drive to keep writing, however, some excellent work managed to emerge from behind the thick walls he had built around himself.

The Spanish Civil War

By the end of 1936, civil war had torn Spain. General Francisco Franco, backed by the dictatorships of Nazi Germany and Fascist Italy, was spearheading a revolution to bring down the working-class Republi-

can party, the Loyalists. Throughout the world, nations took sides as the tug-of-war got rough. Ernest Hemingway supported the Loyalists, saying later, "A writer who will not lie cannot live and work under Fascism."[48] In March 1937 he accepted an assignment from the North American Newspaper Alliance, a news syndicate, to go to Spain to write articles about the Spanish Civil War.

Soon after Hemingway arrived in Madrid, Martha Gellhorn, the writer he had met in Key West, showed up to cover the conflict for *Collier's,* a U.S. magazine. Foreign correspondents in Madrid were in terrible danger. Two of Marty Gellhorn's colleagues were killed. Shaken by air raid sirens and sudden death, Ernest and Marty grew close. By the time they returned to the United States in May 1937, they were in love. Hemingway's marriage to Pauline, the woman for whom he had given up his happy life with Hadley, no longer seemed to matter to him. At the moment, he seemed capable of true loyalty and commitment to one thing only—his creative work. In the States, Ernest and Marty spent increasing amounts of time together even while Ernest and Pauline were still married. In Marty, the intense young author with the loose tumble of golden hair, he

General Francisco Franco reviews his troops. Hemingway covered the Spanish Civil War for an American news syndicate, and his experience served as the inspiration for his most successful novel, For Whom the Bell Tolls.

believed he had found someone who could understand his obsession. After his second divorce, Ernest married Martha Gellhorn on November 21, 1940.

Marty

Hemingway was pleased with himself for winning a young and attractive bride. But he truly appreciated Martha Gellhorn's fine mind and her talent, as well. In the beginning, at least, he saw himself as Marty's mentor, helping her grow in her career. Gellhorn had already published two successful books. When she stalled while writing her third book, *Liana,* a novel that ultimately became a bestseller, Hemingway

coached her through her "writer's block." And he was generous with helpful suggestions about her work. According to writer Michael Reynolds: "After reading one of Martha's stories, Ernest gave her advice about her writing: don't overthink it; get it on paper and have the courage to throw it away if it stinks. A writer, he told her, must push her limits, risking failure in the privacy of her workroom."[49]

Marty appreciated her husband's help. And the teacher-student relationship Hemingway built between them was good for his own writing. Telling Marty to take risks reminded him to be adventurous and innovative in his own work. But, ultimately, Gellhorn would not settle for the role of junior partner in a writing team of Hemingway and Hemingway. She wanted to

During his time as a war correspondent in Spain, Hemingway met and fell in love with fellow writer Martha Gellhorn. Hemingway married "Marty" in November 1940.

write in her own way. And like Ernest himself, she did not hesitate to put her career goals first. As the world's nations skidded faster and faster toward World War II, Ernest and Marty headed for a collision of their own.

Lookout Farm

The couple began their marriage peacefully, however, in a country estate in San Francisco de Paula, Cuba, just outside of Havana. Before the wedding, Marty had found Finca Vigía—"Lookout Farm"—listed in a local classified ad. She rented the ramshackle estate, had it restored and remodeled, and convinced Ernest it would be a wonderful retreat where they could live and write. Hemingway knew Cuba well—his fishing excursions had already taken him there many times while living in Key West. The wealthy author knew that in Cuba, his U.S. taxes as a nonresident would be cheaper. But the appeal of Finca Vigía was more than financial. At the quiet Cuban farm, he could wake at dawn and write through the still, cool mornings, then fish the warm Gulf Stream in the soft afternoon breeze. For a man interested in isolating himself from the rest of the world, it was the perfect retreat.

For decades, until political unrest in Cuba caused him to return to the United States, Finca Vigía became Ernest's home base. Marty had been right; it was a wonderful place to work. In those tranquil mornings, he completed the manuscript of the book that was to be his most successful novel, *For Whom the Bell Tolls.*

For Whom the Bell Tolls

Hemingway chose the title for his next book from the poet John Donne's words: "Any man's death diminishes me, because I am involved in Mankinde. And therefore never send to know for whom the bell tolls [when someone has died]; it tolls for thee." In other words, when one person dies,

everyone is affected. World War II had already ignited the globe by the time *For Whom the Bell Tolls* was published in October 1940. Hemingway's new war novel focused on one of the conflicts that helped trigger World War II—the Spanish Civil War.

Drawing on his experiences in the war-torn country, Hemingway painted a picture of an American soldier, Robert Jordan, who fights side by side with Spanish Loyalists. Jordan's mission, to destroy a bridge, ultimately fails. But through it all, Jordan learns that he loves life and is a part of it, even in the midst of war's devastation. Ultimately, Jordan is fatally wounded by a Fascist bombing attack on his mountain stronghold. As he dies, he praises living:

> If one must die, he thought, and clearly one must, I can die. But I hate it. Dying was nothing and he had no picture of it nor fear of it in his mind. But living was a field of grain blowing in the wind on the side of a hill. Living was a hawk

A Swordlike Edge

In 1954, Hemingway described his writing habits, including the importance of painstaking rewriting, to his colleague and friend A. E. Hotchner, who quotes him in Papa Hemingway.

"I like to start early before I can be distracted by people and events. I've seen every sun rise of my life. I rise at first light . . . and I start by rereading and editing everything I have written to the point I left off. That way I go through a book I'm writing several hundred times. Then I go right on, no p—ing around, crumbling up paper, pacing because I always stop at a point where I know precisely what's going to happen next. So I don't have to crank up every day. Most writers slough off the toughest but most important part of their trade—editing their stuff, honing it and honing it until it gets an edge like the bullfighter's *estoque,* the killing sword."

in the sky. Living was an earthen jar of water in the dust of threshing, with the grain flailed out and the chaff blowing. Living was a horse between your legs and a carbine under one leg and a hill and a valley and a stream with trees along it and the far side of the valley and the hills beyond.[50]

The novel was Hemingway's longest and most complex thus far. According to Reynolds, its richness was the direct result of everything Hemingway had learned about and lived through:

To create his characters, he needed all those Spanish days . . . studying the bullring and the faces surrounding it. He needed the African book to learn about moving people through terrain. He needed all those experiments with structure before he could write this story which has within it several other stories, each in a separate voice. He needed his affair with Martha before he could write of his fictional Maria. He needed the strength and purpose of Pauline to create the older woman, Pilar, whose name once belonged to her. He needed to watch the Italian bombers on the Tortosa road before he could describe the bombing of the lonely hilltop.[51]

Finca Vigía, or "Lookout Farm," was Hemingway's estate in San Francisco de Paula, Cuba. This is where Hemingway completed the manuscript for the novel For Whom the Bell Tolls.

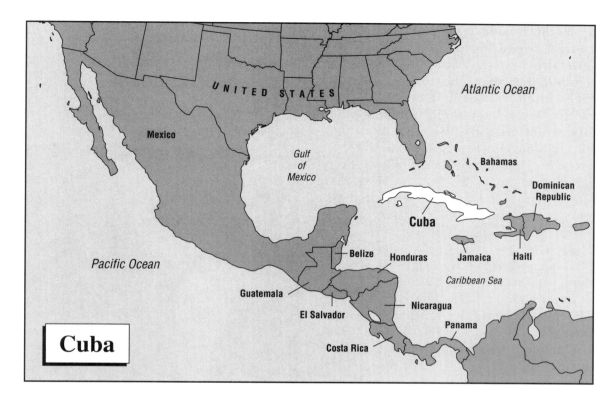

Cuba

Hemingway had funneled the pains and joys of his life to date into the novel. He later said the message of *For Whom the Bell Tolls* was that no man is an island—all humans are connected by a common thread. Hemingway, whose self-absorption was isolating him from others, seemed to be well aware that he should not cut himself off from his fellow human beings. But, stubbornly, as though his life and work depended on it, he continued to try to close himself off from others as the war years continued.

Death of a Friend and Rival

Ernest had no way of knowing when he sent F. Scott Fitzgerald a copy of this latest book, inscribed "To Scott with affection and esteem Ernest," that his friend would soon be dead. On November 8, 1940, Scott wrote Hemingway to thank him for the book and to praise it. The novel was selling wildly. Scott complimented his old friend on its success a little sadly: "I envy you like hell and there is no irony in this. . . . I envy you the time it will give you to do what you want."[52]

That was to be his last letter to Ernest. Scott was living in Hollywood, hiring himself out as a film script writer. But he was not making much money. At a time when he should have been enjoying the same fame and good fortune as Ernest Hemingway, Fitzgerald had to scramble to earn a living. The world seemed to have forgotten him. A month after receiving Hemingway's gift, Fitzgerald died in Hollywood of a heart attack. He was only in his forties.

The two writers had held on to their unusual friendship in spite of their disagreements. In fact, they had more in common than they realized. Their personalities often clashed, but they both confronted similar emotional problems that threatened their art. And they both had admired one another's work as well as criticized it. Hemingway would always be a fierce defender of his favorite Fitzgerald novel, *Tender Is the Night,* published six years before the author's early death. In time, readers would rediscover Fitzgerald's books. The same melancholy man who died a has-been would be studied in classrooms along with his wild friend Ernest.

Fitzgerald had been right—Hemingway had earned the money to do whatever he liked. The royalties from *For Whom the Bell Tolls* allowed the Hemingways to buy their farmhouse in Cuba instead of rent it. The couple spent the first three years of World War II in the country hideaway. Unfortunately, Martha was soon to find it a prison rather than a refuge. Ernest had started drinking heavily, staying out late for drunken parties in Havana bars and then lying to her about where he had been. He lounged around barefoot, in faded swimming trunks and sweaty shirts. He was never available when she needed him. He argued with her in public. The dozens of cats he fed and allowed indoors made messes all over the house. Gellhorn was angry and worried.

Hemingway's actions gave the impression he did not care much about being a husband. His self-involvement kept him from contributing much to the marriage. He no longer gave his wife writing advice. He spent little time with her. They no longer seemed to share common goals. Gellhorn was especially surprised and dis-

In December 1940, F. Scott Fitzgerald died of a heart attack in Hollywood, California. In contrast to Hemingway's soaring success, Fitzgerald was fading into obscurity at the time of his death.

appointed to learn that he did not seem excited about getting involved with the war effort. When they had fallen in love during the Spanish Civil War, Hemingway had been an enthusiastic supporter of the Loyalist cause. His political efforts had attracted her—he had seemed to share her concern about the world and its problems. Now, even though all Europe was at war, her husband seemed to care only about himself, she thought. Soon Marty began accepting journalism assignments that kept her away from Finca Vigía—and Ernest— for weeks. Gellhorn wanted to help the world with her writing talent. But she also wanted to avoid her husband's cold rudeness.

War Games

Although Hemingway was withdrawing from his wife, he was still interested in helping the United States with the war effort in his own unusual way. He was a rich man with an expensive plaything—the *Pilar,* the powerful diesel fishing boat he and Pauline had bought after returning from their safari. And even though Hemingway was in his early forties, he still liked adventure. Filled with enthusiasm and patriotism, he approached the U.S. Navy with what he saw as an inspired idea. He would arm the *Pilar* with machine guns and grenades and cruise the waters off Cuba with a crew of civilian sailors, scouting for enemy submarines. Hemingway figured he and his crew could pose as marine biologists. If they sighted a Nazi sub, the *Pilar* would open fire.

Because of the need for counterspying in the area, the Navy took him up on the scheme. Hemingway and his crew, calling themselves the Crook Factory, spent the summer of 1942 putting about in the ocean looking for submarines to sink. His face got so sunburned it hurt to shave, and he grew a bushy beard. He was having a great time, but his wife was not impressed. She found the whole idea of the Crook Factory silly. Ernest was drinking far too much and writing far too little, Marty told him. In her frustration, she went farther than that. According to biographer Carlos Baker, "She . . . enraged him by suggesting that the *Pilar*'s . . . patrols were only an excuse to get rationed gasoline so that he . . . could go on fishing while the rest of the civilized world fought, suffered, and died."[53]

While Hemingway played war games, Gellhorn finished her third novel. Not long after, Hemingway left on a three-month fishing trip. Gellhorn did not wait patiently for his return. Instead, she got on a boat headed for London to cover the war at close quarters for *Collier's* magazine. She was still overseas at Christmas, and Hemingway spent the holiday at Finca Vigía alone. Feeling lonely and abandoned, he cursed what he saw as her selfishness. Gellhorn tried to reassure him she still loved him, but Hemingway sent her angry cablegrams: "ARE YOU A WAR CORRESPONDENT OR WIFE IN MY BED?"[54]

Hemingway wanted to be left alone, but he still wanted a wife who would be a loyal, loving companion. He convinced himself that Marty's desire to have her own career was interfering with being a good wife. In an interview for a popular magazine, Hemingway managed to sound supportive of his wife's ambition while still implying that she spent more time working than she should:

> When she is at the front or getting there, she will get up earlier, travel longer and faster and go where no other woman can get and where few could stick it out if they did. . . . She gets to the place, gets the story, writes it and comes home. That last is the best part.[55]

But when Marty did come home, Ernest punished her for her absence. In his self-centeredness, he seemed to think his own needs should always come first. Gellhorn recalled one of his unfair outbursts:

Scientific Sombreros

Norberto Fuentes, a Cuban author and journalist who gained access from the Cuban government to Hemingway's books, papers, and files, wrote a book recounting the American author's years at Finca Vigía called Hemingway in Cuba. *In this passage, he discusses Hemingway's antisubmarine mission and how it was translated into fiction in* Islands in the Stream, *a Hemingway novel published after his death.*

"The *Pilar*'s becoming part of American Intelligence caused the boat to be completely refitted . . . it was overhauled and its old gas engines renovated . . . carpenters built some glass holders, which were really to be used to store hand grenades out of sight. . . .

The sign installed on the *Pilar* after its renovation work read *American Museum of Natural History*. It was meant to confuse the enemy and give the impression that the *Pilar* was a peaceful vessel on a scientific investigation.

Their scientific classification amused the crew of the *Pilar* and was the subject of many jokes. They classified everything on board—even their hats—as 'scientific.' The hats, wide-brimmed native *sombreros*, were used as a protection from the sun, since there was very little cover on the *Pilar*'s decks. The business of the 'scientific sombreros' was later used by Hemingway in *Islands in the Stream*.

Years after through the magic of fiction, Hemingway accomplished what had never happened in real life. If his Nazi submarine hunt never amounted to much, in *Islands in the Stream* he succeeded in engaging the German boats in combat, using all his war potential on an equal basis. If in real life the hull of the *Pilar* could not withstand the installation of the two .50-caliber antiaircraft guns (instead there were magnetic mines, dynamite charges and antitank guns), in the book it easily accommodated two—one foreship and one astern."

Ernest began at once to rave at me, the word is not too strong. He woke me when I was trying to sleep to bully, snarl, mock—my crime really was to have been at war when he had not. . . . I only wanted excitement and danger, I had no responsibility to anyone, I was selfish beyond belief . . . it never stopped and believe me, it was fierce and ugly.[56]

When Gellhorn invited her husband to come to England with her, Hemingway decided to take her up on the offer. He was finally ready to write about the war, but he deliberately chose to do so in a way that put Gellhorn out of a job. He contacted the same magazine she worked for, *Collier's,* and offered his services. They hired him to report on the Royal Air Force. According to the rules of the U.S. Press Corps, each magazine was allowed only one frontline correspondent. Marty was out, her husband was in. But Gellhorn was determined to go overseas anyway and keep writing about the war.

When they were both in New York preparing to leave for England, Marty warned Ernest that their marriage was in danger unless he stopped mistreating her. He ignored her and boarded a plane that had been arranged for him without offering her a seat. She had to catch a ride on a freighter carrying a cargo of dynamite. For the whole seventeen-day voyage she worried that the ship would blow up. And when she arrived, she was surrounded by British reporters who told her Ernest had gashed his scalp in a drunken car crash af-

ter a party. She went to his hospital room, which was littered with empty liquor bottles smuggled in by his drinking buddies, and told him their five-year marriage was through.

Mary Welsh

Ernest was upset, but apparently not very deeply. He had never allowed himself to become truly attached to his independent wife. As soon as he had arrived in England, in fact, Hemingway had already struck up a friendship with another American journalist, Mary Welsh Monks. The thirty-six-year-old feature writer for *Time* magazine was staying at the same hotel as the Hemingways. Even though they were both married, Hemingway lost no time in telling the bright, petite woman that he wanted to marry her someday. Her own marriage was faltering, and Hemingway's attentions were flattering. Like Martha Gellhorn, Mary Welsh also visited Ernest's hospital

When Hemingway went to Europe to cover World War II for Collier's *magazine his five-year marriage to Martha was in trouble. His wild antics and self-absorbed behavior eventually caused his third marriage to collapse.*

room. But instead of angry accusations, she brought him a bouquet of tulips.

By 1946, Mary Welsh had become the fourth Mrs. Hemingway. Ernest, forty-six years old, was looking for a loyal companion. In a fateful turn of events, he did something that inspired Mary's firm devotion—he saved her life. After they were married, an ectopic pregnancy (an unsuccessful pregnancy in its earliest stages) caused Mary to rupture internally while they were vacationing in Sun Valley, Idaho. She fainted and rapidly lost blood. Finally, the doctors gave up on saving her. But Hemingway, instinctively calling on knowledge he had gained as a doctor's son, shouted sharp orders to the nurses. He took over the plasma administration

While he was covering WW II in Europe Hemingway met American journalist Mary Welsh Monks. In 1946 Mary became Ernest's fourth wife.

himself, revived Mary, and demanded that the doctors operate. According to biographer Bernice Kert:

> No one who witnessed the crisis had anything but tremendous respect for Ernest's quick action. The anesthetist, the doctors, and Mary herself knew that he had saved her life. As disappointed as she was to lose her baby, Mary's appreciation for Ernest seemed to swell into an everlasting and unshakable trust. . . . She had seen him at his solid best—quick-thinking, modest, effective, and it put into permanent perspective the occasional bullying, the vanity, the sudden gusts of cruelty.[57]

Hemingway resumed his relaxed, isolated life in Cuba with the new bride he called "Small Friend." Welsh tried to take good care of her moody, often unpleasant husband, whose car accident had left him with terrible headaches and hearing loss. She put the farmhouse in order and even learned to fish, going along on his excursions aboard the *Pilar*. But although Hemingway called her his friend, he did not treat her as an equal. Whenever he had business matters to discuss with colleagues, for example, he asked her to leave the room.

Mary was not happy with such treatment, but she put up with it. Her devotion to her husband even led her to tolerate his friendship with an attractive eighteen-year-old girl the Hemingways met in Venice, Adriana Ivancich. Ernest, the father of three sons, had always wanted a daughter—he even started calling most women he met "Daughter." But his feelings toward the brunette teenager were more than merely fatherly. Although Adriana considered him just a friend, Hemingway had a crush on

Though he was divorced from their mothers, Ernest always saw his sons on a regular basis.

her. They talked for hours, with Ernest doing most of the talking, to the disapproval of Adriana's strict mother. However Mary felt about it privately, she did not interfere with her husband's gentle flirtation.

Across the River and into the Trees

Back in Cuba, always measuring his own self-worth against his success as a writer, Hemingway tried to stay ahead of his reputation, suspecting that his critics were eager to see him topple. Now that the war was over, he needed another worthy focus for his writing efforts. Over the course of

several years, he had been shaping three linked narratives about the sea, but had never finished them. He considered tinkering with them again.

During this unproductive time, a profile of Hemingway came out in the *New Yorker* magazine that opened him up to ridicule. The Hemingways had allowed a journalist acquaintance, Lillian Ross, to follow them around for two days, taking detailed notes on whatever Hemingway said or did. As it turned out, he joked drunkenly with friends at dinner and went clothes shopping for a trip to Italy. Under Ross's observing eye, Mary Hemingway comes across as a patient baby-sitter to a childish middle-aged man. Ross wrote later that she was trying to convey the famous author's "enormous spirit of fun." But many *New Yorker* readers did not find her controversial portrait of Hemingway so funny. Instead, they thought he was boastful and boring.

That same year Hemingway published his long-awaited new novel, *Across the River and into the Trees.* Part of the novel was inspired by his friendship with Adriana Ivancich. Fittingly, one of her sketches adorned the book's jacket. The novel described the passionate love of a middle-aged, ailing American colonel for a young Italian countess. It was his first published novel in a decade. It had been almost twenty-five years since the thundering success of *The Sun Also Rises.*

Across the River disappointed the critics. They wondered whether Hemingway had lost his touch, or if perhaps his macho characters had simply gone out of style. Adjectives that book reviewers used to criticize Hemingway's latest novel included "tired," "embarrassing," and "distressing." Despite the bashing from critics, the novel sold briskly to fans hungry for more Hemingway.

A Different Story

But Hemingway suspected there was a better book in him, a different kind of story altogether. In January 1952, his daily writing took on a sudden surge of energy. He took up one of the three sea stories he had been working on before *Across the River* was published, tentatively titled "The Sea in Being." Swiftly and with confidence, he sculpted a story about an old Cuban fisherman and a giant marlin, basing the action on a situation he had heard about back in 1935.

Hemingway's absorption in the story of the man he named Santiago and his quest was so complete that instead of his usual five hundred words per day, he was averaging twice that amount. As was his custom, he wrote standing up, his typewriter perched on top of a bookcase. According to Baker: "Ernest could never afterwards quite express his astonishment at the speed and ease with which the story of Santiago had spun loose from the cocoon where it had lain waiting for sixteen years." [58]

The story, retitled *The Old Man and the Sea,* would become Hemingway's most widely acclaimed and enduring work. He showed the manuscript, shorter than his usual novels, to his publisher and select friends. Each person was struck by its mysterious, almost mythic quality. It sounded different from anything else he had ever written. Hemingway could feel the power of his own accomplishment. He was very pleased with himself for proving that, as a writer to be reckoned with, he was far from through. According to biographer James R. Mellow, Hemingway explained when he sent the manuscript to Scribner's in March 1952, "Publishing it now will get rid of the school of criticism that I am through as a writer. It will destroy the school of criticism that claims I can write about nothing except myself and my own experiences." [59] Through Scribner's, he began negotiating with magazines to publish the story in installments. He had originally intended to publish all three sea narratives as one book, but soon decided that *The Old Man and the Sea* was powerful enough to stand alone.

In the middle of his excited negotiations, Hemingway received the news that his mother, Grace, had died at the age of seventy-nine. Suddenly, despite his old feelings of anger at Grace, childhood

"The Part That Doesn't Show"

In an interview for the Paris Review, *writer George Plimpton grills Hemingway on his writing methods and theories. In this excerpt Hemingway gives an idea of his "iceberg" method as he used it when writing his highly successful* The Old Man and the Sea, *a simple story with much—like an iceberg—hidden beneath the surface. This excerpt comes from "An Interview with Ernest Hemingway," by George Plimpton, collected in* Ernest Hemingway, *edited by Harold Bloom.*

"INTERVIEWER: So when you're not writing, you remain constantly the observer, looking for something which can be of use.

HEMINGWAY: Surely. If a writer stops observing he is finished. But he does not have to observe consciously or think how it will be useful. Perhaps that would be true at the beginning. But later everything he sees goes into the great reserve of things he knows or has seen. . . . I always try to write on the principle of the iceberg. There is seven eighths of it under water for every part that shows. Anything you know you can eliminate and it only strengthens your iceberg. It is the part that doesn't show. . . . *The Old Man and the Sea* could have been over a thousand pages long and had every character in the village in it and all the processes of how they made their living, were born, educated, bore children, etc. That is done excellently and well by other writers. In writing you are limited by what has already been done satisfactorily. So I have tried to learn to do something else. First I have tried to eliminate everything unnecessary to conveying experience to the reader so that after he or she has read something it will become a part of his or her experience and seem actually to have happened. This is very hard to do and I've worked at it very hard.

Anyway, to skip to how it is done, I had unbelievable luck this time and could convey the experience completely and have it be one that no one had ever conveyed. . . . I've seen the marlin mate and know about that. So I leave that out. I've seen a school (or pod) of more than fifty sperm whales in that same stretch of water and once harpooned one nearly sixty feet in length and lost him. So I left that out. All the stories I know from the fishing village I leave out. But the knowledge is what makes the underwater part of the iceberg."

memories of how happy they had been as a family came flooding back to him. Hemingway remained in Cuba during the funeral. But he asked his parish priest in San Francisco de Paula, the village near Finca Vigía, to say a Mass in her memory.

Grace Hall Hemingway, who always maintained that she was proud of all her children, did not live to enjoy the renewed respect that the publication of *The Old Man and the Sea* would bring her famous son. But Hemingway had, in large part, her example of tireless dedication and creative enthusiasm to thank for his impressive achievement. At her son's request, on the day she was buried in Illinois, the church bell in San Francisco de Paula tolled for Grace at dawn.

Chapter

5 Redemption

After the artistic breakthrough of *The Old Man and the Sea,* the early 1950s became a time of artistic and personal redemption for Hemingway. He wrote one of his most uplifting and enduring works, regained his public's respect, and won two coveted awards. It was a time of triumph and recognition. His efforts to stay on top had paid off. The author's exclusive focus on himself and his work had taken its toll on his personal life. But at last Hemingway could begin to feel he had come to terms with his mistakes and rise above his past artistic and personal failures. His successes energized him, but they also became a pressing challenge to live up to.

The Old Man and the Sea

After the publication of *The Old Man and the Sea* in 1952, its meaning was much discussed and debated. But whatever it meant, there was no doubt it was loved. *Life* magazine printed pages of letters from readers praising it. No book of Hemingway's seems to have hit more readers harder than *The Old Man and the Sea.* And yet no work of his appears—at least on the surface—simpler. Told with the measured plainness of scripture, the novella (short

novel) recounts the story of a Cuban fisherman and his three-day ordeal battling a huge marlin far out in the Gulf. The old man, Santiago, is down on his luck. He has not caught a single big fish in eighty-four days, and he is slowly wasting away. His friend, a young boy, still believes in him and tries to encourage him.

Santiago's struggle ends in failure—he kills the marlin but it is too enormous to fit in the boat. Before he can tow it all the way in to shore, it is ripped apart by hungry sharks. But Santiago's refusal to give up hope expresses Hemingway's belief in the human spirit's staying power against all odds. In the novella, he maintains, "A man can be destroyed, but not defeated."[60] Santiago's struggles redeem his worth as a human being. This was Hemingway's personal code, as well. As long as he could keep fighting, he would stay worthy of respect.

A Religious Message?

The story meant different things to different people. Many readers believed they saw Christian symbolism in the story of the old fisherman. Although he was a practicing Catholic, having converted to the faith before he married Pauline Pfeiffer, Ernest protested that he had not intended any religious references. In fact, he had often expressed mixed feelings about organized religion. Nevertheless, after Santiago groans "Ay" at the ominous approach of a pair of sharks, the narrative continues, "There is no translation for this word, and

In 1952 Hemingway's most critically acclaimed work was published. The Old Man and the Sea *is a tale about an old Cuban fisherman who battles a giant marlin in the Gulf of Mexico.*

perhaps it is just a noise such as a man might make, involuntarily, feeling the nail go through his hands and into the wood." [61] The image calls to mind Christ's crucifixion, as though Hemingway were comparing Santiago's ordeal to the suffering of Jesus. Both Christian and Jewish clergy began preaching sermons using *The Old Man and the Sea* as their text.

One of Hemingway's most famous contemporaries, the Nobel Prize–winning author William Faulkner, also believed that *The Old Man and the Sea* sent readers a religious message. In a review in a literary magazine, Faulkner wrote:

> This time [Hemingway] discovered God, a creator. Until now, his men and women had made themselves, shaped themselves out of their own clay; their victories and defeats were at the hands of each other, just to prove to themselves or one another how tough they could be. But this time, he wrote about pity: about something somewhere that . . . made them all and loved them all and pitied them all. [62]

To Faulkner, Hemingway's book expressed the belief that man's fate could not be controlled by man alone. It depended instead upon the mercy of a higher power.

Hemingway, who was receiving eighty to ninety letters a day praising *The Old Man and the Sea,* was a little impatient with all the speculation. He avoided analyzing the book's meaning or the source of his inspiration to write it. Instead, in a later interview, he chalked up the whole thing to luck: "The luck was that I had a good man and a good boy and lately writers have forgotten there still are such things. Then the ocean is worth writing about just as man is. So I was lucky there." [63] While readers tried

A Code for Heroes

Hemingway scholar Philip Young, in his discussion reprinted in Readings on Ernest Hemingway, *published by Greenhaven Press, describes the Hemingway "code hero." This hero, appearing repeatedly in his fiction, reflects Hemingway's ideal way of responding to the world with courage and honor. Santiago, in* The Old Man and the Sea, *is a "code hero," Young believes.*

"There is in Hemingway a consistent character. . . . This figure is not Hemingway himself in disguise. . . . Indeed he is to be sharply distinguished from the hero, for he comes to balance the hero's deficiencies, to correct his stance. We generally . . . call this man the 'code hero'—this because he represents a code according to which the hero, if he could attain it, would be able to live properly in the world of violence, disorder, and misery to which he has been introduced and which he inhabits. The code hero, then, offers up . . . certain principles of honor, courage, and endurance which in a life of tension and pain make a man a man, as we say, and enable him to conduct himself well in the losing battle that is life. He shows, in the author's famous phrase for it, 'grace under pressure.'

The finest and best known of these code heroes appears . . . in [*The Old Man and the Sea*]. He is old Santiago. . . . The chief point about him is that he behaves perfectly—honorably, with great courage and endurance—while losing to the sharks the giant fish he has caught. This, to epitomize the message the code hero always brings, is life: you lose, of course; what counts is how you conduct yourself while you are being destroyed."

to peer below the surface of the tale for hidden meanings, its author insisted that its simple plot, characters, and setting spoke for themselves. Nevertheless, a title Hemingway had originally considered for the book gives a clue to the story's meaning to its author: *The Dignity of Man.*

In December, filmmaker Leland Hayward approached Ernest about making a play out of *The Old Man and the Sea,* to be followed by a film version starring Spencer Tracy. It was not the first time Hemingway's work had been adapted to the movie screen, but it was to be the fanciest production to date. Because Hayward wanted the fishing scenes to look realistic, he asked Ernest to fish for shark in the Caribbean and giant marlin in Peru while being filmed by a Hollywood crew. Although the author himself would not appear in the movie, edited versions of the fishing footage might. Ernest accepted

In addition to having The Old Man and the Sea *turned into a movie starring the legendary Spencer Tracy (pictured on the set with Hemingway), Hemingway won the coveted Pulitzer Prize for Fiction. Though he downplayed the event, Hemingway was jubilant that his talent had finally been officially recognized.*

with pleasure—the deal would bring him a lot of money, as well as the adventure of the fishing excursions themselves.

The Pulitzer Prize

In the waters near his home, on May 4, 1953, Ernest was out sportfishing on the *Pilar.* Over the ship's radio, the six o'clock news broadcast murmured in the background. Suddenly the author was surprised to hear his own name over the airwaves. He turned up the volume and discovered he had just won the Pulitzer Prize for Fiction for *The Old Man and the Sea.* He was jubilant.

He had waited a long time for this important honor. Many of his supporters believed that Hemingway should have won the Pulitzer for *For Whom the Bell Tolls* more than a decade earlier. But, in 1940, when the book appeared, the Pulitzer Prize advisory board had voted not to award a prize

for fiction at all. The decision implied that they did not think anything published that year was good enough for the honor. After that painful rejection of what many believed to be his best book to date, Hemingway had pretended that he did not care at all about winning awards. Now, at last, at age fifty-three, he had won official recognition for his writing. His single-minded dedication to his craft had reaped a tangible reward. Jokingly, he called it the Pullover Prize, trying not to show how proud he really was.

Back to Africa

Energized by the great news, Ernest and Mary Hemingway prepared to travel to Africa on safari. Hemingway was excited about returning to big-game hunting. Editors at *Life* magazine were pleased as well—they hired the famous author to write a series of articles about his upcoming adventures. In the summer of 1953, after a detour in Spain where Hemingway showed his wife the places that had inspired him when writing *For Whom the Bell Tolls,* the couple took off by steamship down the coast of East Africa to the city of Mombasa, Kenya.

Unfortunately, after this particular adventure, Hemingway would never be quite the same. The incredible disaster he was to suffer topped off a series of accidents he had survived since young manhood. Hemingway would barely make it through the harrowing African experience alive. Momentarily, in fact, the world would believe that he was dead.

Two Crashes

On January 21, 1954, the Hemingways took off from Entebbe, Uganda, near the shore of Lake Victoria, in a light plane. Their pilot was a young man named Roy Marsh. Mary wanted to take aerial photographs of Murchison Falls, north of Lake Albert in Uganda. Flying low, Marsh struck a telegraph wire. The plane's propeller bent. Marsh had to make a forced landing. When the plane jolted to the ground, Mary injured her chest and Ernest hurt his right shoulder. Marsh sent out a distress call on the plane radio. After a while, they

In January 1954 Mary and Ernest Hemingway took a trip that would forever alter their lives. While traveling in Africa their plane crashed and the world believed that the award-winning author was dead.

were picked up by a river steamer that took them to the town of Butiaba, Uganda.

The pilot's distress signal had already reached Nairobi, Kenya. Its recipients believed that the group had not survived the crash. The false report that the famous Ernest Hemingway had been killed promptly circled the globe. Meanwhile, another pilot offered to fly the three accident victims back to Entebbe. They would have to take off from a bumpy, unmaintained runway, but they accepted. Halfway down the runway, flames erupted from both plane engines. The cockpit doors jammed. Ernest, Mary, and Roy Marsh were trapped inside the plane. Finally, Marsh managed to kick out a window and pulled Mary out of the cockpit. Ernest, striking with his head and injured shoulder, battered his way through the door on the other side of the flaming plane.

Hemingway's head was gashed and bleeding. He had also suffered internal injuries—no one knew at first how severe. His wife had wrenched her knee. Since Butiaba had no medical facilities, the Hemingways had to hire a car and ride the 150 miles to Entebbe. During a pause in the excruciating journey, Mary was able to cable her family that she and Ernest had in fact survived, despite reports to the contrary. Ernest and Pauline's older son, Patrick, flew to meet them in Entebbe. They made it to Nairobi. Mary had broken some ribs. But her husband's injuries were extensive.

The damages included a concussion; a collapsed lower intestine; a ruptured liver, spleen, and kidney; a crushed vertebra; a sprained right arm and shoulder; a sprained left leg; and first-degree burns on his face, arms, and head. Despite the beating he had taken, he managed to sit up in his hospital bed and read through all the congratulatory telegrams that poured in from throughout the globe from people

After their plane went down in Africa, Ernest and his wife miraculously survived a second plane crash. In addition to the many injuries Ernest accumulated in the plane mishaps he was seriously burned while fighting a brushfire in a fishing camp.

who were glad he was still alive. He also studied with great interest all the obituaries that had appeared about him in countless newspapers before word had reached the world that he had not been killed after all.

Hemingway enjoyed the irony of reading his own death notices. But he resented that some people seemed to think he had a death wish. He later remarked: "In all obituaries, or almost all, it was emphasized that I had sought death all my life. Can one imagine that if a man sought death all of his life he could not have found her before the age of 54?"[64] Far from having a death wish, the author seemed determined to cling to life when others might have let go from sheer exhaustion. Returning to his writing as a source of strength, Hemingway steamrolled ahead. In the hospital, he dictated a fifteen-thousand-word article for *Look* magazine about the horrible experience.

Unbelievably, misfortune struck a third time. Although he was not yet healed, in late February, Hemingway insisted on joining his oldest son at a fishing camp on the Kenya coast. While the others were fishing, a brushfire started near the camp. It had only been about a month since his accident. Despite his fragile health, the author insisted on playing hero and joined others fighting the blaze. But he was still weak and dizzy. Wobbling on his feet, he tumbled into some burning brush and was seriously burned over most of his body before he was dragged to safety. Mary persuaded him to get out of Africa before he self-destructed.

Hemingway rested in Venice, Italy. He then returned home to San Francisco de Paula, Cuba, where he tried to stick to doctors' orders to drink less, sleep longer, and eat better. For the time being, he put serious writing on hold. But he couldn't shut off the flow of words that sustained him in both good and bad times. He wrote letter after letter to friends.

Hemingway's close call seemed to have mellowed him, if only somewhat. He embarked on a careful program of physical training, including daily workouts in his swimming pool at Finca Vigía. Soon he was well enough to fulfill his obligation to the Hollywood director who wanted his help with the filming of *The Old Man and the Sea*. Every day, he went out with a camera crew and fished for marlin at the wheel of the *Pilar,* finally succeeding in getting the filmmakers the realistic footage they needed.

Despite his brushes with death, Hemingway was hardly finished yet with the life he had always lived with such gusto. His bushy white beard and the weight he had lost because of his injuries made him look older than he was. But he was determined to work his body and mind back to health. Yet, according to biographer Carlos Baker, "The crash at Butiaba and the fire at Shimoni had . . . left him no more than a shadow of his former vigor."[65] Hemingway's rehabilitation would take time away from his writing. But whether his injuries would also affect the quality of his writing remained to be seen.

The Nobel Prize

The year that had begun disastrously wound up on a high note. In October 1954, Ernest Hemingway won the Nobel Prize for Literature, the most prestigious honor a writer can achieve. Early in the morning of October 28, the United Press newspaper service phoned him with the news. Mary was still

In October 1954 Ernest Hemingway won the highest honor a writer can receive, the Nobel Prize for Literature. He could not go to Sweden to receive the honor because he had not fully recovered from his injuries.

asleep. According to biographer James R. Mellow, Hemingway was thrilled: "'My kitten, my kitten,' he told Mary, waking her, 'I've got that thing.'"[66] He was only the fifth American to win the prize—William Faulkner had received it in 1949.

Hemingway had not recovered completely enough from his injuries to go to Stockholm, Sweden, to accept his award in person. Instead, he wrote and tape-recorded a message of acceptance. In it, he commented that a writer "does his work alone and if he is a good enough writer he must face eternity, or the lack of it, each day."[67] As Hemingway knew, writing well was a hard and nerve-wracking job, but it could be a deeply rewarding one. Hemingway saw the public validation of the Nobel Prize award as a sign that, despite his personal and professional failings, he had redeemed himself as worthy in the eyes of the world. Because he measured his own self-esteem against the yardstick of public

Fighting the Good Fight

On October 28, 1954, the Swedish Academy awarded Hemingway the Nobel Prize for Literature, considered the highest honor a writer can receive. In Ernest Hemingway: A Life Story, *Carlos Baker quotes from the Academy's announcement.*

"For his powerful style-forming mastery of the art of modern narration, as most recently evinced in *The Old Man and the Sea* . . . Hemingway's earlier writings displayed brutal, cynical and callous signs which may be considered at variance with the Nobel Prize requirements for a work of ideal tendencies. But on the other hand he also possesses a heroic pathos which forms the basic element of this awareness of life, a manly love of danger and adventure, with a natural admiration of every individual who fights the good fight in a world of reality overshadowed by violence and death."

approval, the award was a comfort. But it also represented the end of a journey—he could hardly climb any higher than this. Instead, he balanced on top of a remote pinnacle of success few others had ever reached. The only place to go next was downhill.

Shadows in the Midst of Success

Hemingway's parents had both passed away before they could share his crowning achievement. Hemingway's ex-wife Pauline had also died by the time Hemingway won the Nobel Prize. In fact, both Grace and Pauline had died in the same year, 1952. Pauline's sudden death, at the age of only fifty-six, was caused by a rare, undiagnosed tumor of the adrenal gland. When she died, Hemingway wrote his publisher, Charles Scribner: "I loved her very much for many years and the hell with her faults."[68] The former couple had remained in touch about their sons, Patrick and Gregory. Her absence during his life's most important event to date only made Hemingway more keenly aware that life itself was fleeting, bittersweet, and unpredictable.

In addition, Pauline Hemingway's death triggered an estrangement between father and son that resembled Hemingway's own fury at his mother after his father's suicide. Pauline's illness had been aggravated by her emotional upset over their son Gregory's arrest in Los Angeles on drug charges. After the publication of *The Old Man and the Sea,* Gregory battered his father with angry letters, accusing him of accelerating Pauline's illness with their ar-guing (Pauline had phoned Ernest for help when Gregory got into trouble, and they had quarreled over the matter). Gregory also resented his father's lack of attention when he was growing up. In his letters, Gregory criticized the book most readers were praising, calling *The Old Man and the Sea* sentimental garbage.

Gregory Hemingway's bitterness toward his father lasted a year or two. By the time his father had accepted the Nobel Prize, however, they had patched up their differences. Their reconciliation heartened Hemingway, who wanted to see himself as a good father and a good husband, despite the track record of the past. The winning of the Nobel Prize was an opportunity to usher in a time of personal, as

When Pauline Pfeiffer died in 1952, Gregory Hemingway (pictured) blamed his father for his mother's untimely death.

Facing Eternity Each Day

When Hemingway received the Nobel Prize in October 1954, he was still recovering from injuries suffered in two plane crashes while on safari. This passage is excerpted from Hemingway's brief acceptance speech, read in his absence at the Nobel Prize awards banquet and quoted in Carlos Baker's Ernest Hemingway: A Life Story.

"Writing, at its best, is a lonely life. Organizations for writers palliate the writer's loneliness but I doubt if they improve his writing . . . for he does his work alone and if he is a good enough writer he must face eternity, or the lack of it, each day. For a true writer each book should be a new beginning where he tries again for something that is beyond attainment. He should always try for something that has never been done or that others have tried and failed. Then sometimes, with great luck, he will succeed. . . . It is because we have had such great writers in the past that a writer is driven far out past where he can go, out to where no one can help him."

well as professional, growth for a man who had devoted most of his emotions and his energy to his work alone.

Shaky Health

But Hemingway needed to improve his shaky physical health before he could consider any psychological improvements. In the fall of 1955, he caught a cold while accepting an award at a Havana sports arena. Two days later, his foot swelled and he developed a severe kidney infection. The illness sent him to bed for more than a month. Other health problems followed.

His temper suffered along with his health. Even visiting the movie set of *The Old Man and the Sea* infuriated him. Irritated by director Leland Hayward's casting choices (he thought the boy chosen to play Santiago's friend looked like a tadpole), Hemingway quarreled with people on the set, including the star, Spencer Tracy. After two weeks he wrote a friend that he had decided never to get involved in movies again.

Hemingway did not take a break from writing during this time of physical recovery. Instead of enjoying his recent literary achievement, he was already looking to the next project. He felt anxious whenever he was not writing, as though something terrible might happen if his words stopped flowing. In addition to working in fits and starts on the draft of another book about Africa, the author finished several short stories. But he was unhappy with the quality and quantity of his work, taking out his frustration on other successful writers he had set himself in competition with, including William Faulkner and Irving Stone.

Hemingway and Stone met on a cruise to Europe. Hemingway was incensed when the author of *Lust for Life* and *The Agony and the Ecstasy* jokingly pointed out that the ship's bookstore had nine of Stone's books on display, but only three of Hemingway's. Unable to let this inequity pass, Hemingway had a little word with the management. By the next morning, the bookstore had changed its display to six Hemingway titles and six Stone titles.

More health trouble, this time a liver problem and high blood pressure, kept Hemingway from taking a return trip to Africa in the fall of 1956. He was impatient with doctors' orders to stop drinking and eat a strict diet. He complained to a friend that he felt nervous, hungry, and irritable. Unlike his father, whose depression had worsened at the prospect of following a health regimen, Hemingway dutifully followed his doctors' program. But his continuing health problems discouraged him.

Hemingway managed to stay on his best behavior until a return trip to Spain in the fall of 1956. He went there to research bullfighting for a *Life* magazine article he was writing. On this trip, he attended every bullfight starring Antonio Ordoñez. The young matador was the son of another famous matador, Cayetano Ordoñez, who had been the model for Hemingway's Romero in *The Sun Also Rises*. Caught up in the seductive energy of Spain at fiesta time, Hemingway decided he was tired of following doctors' orders. The nostalgic trip was flawed by his return to heavy drinking. Older and less steady on his feet, he could no longer tramp from cantina to cantina. Instead, he sat in the hotel bar and drank himself into a daze, telling stories to whoever would listen until his companions finally coaxed him into going to bed.

Fortunately, when the Hemingways returned to Finca Vigía in early 1957, Ernest quit drinking again, promising Mary it would be for good this time. He also started taking the medicine prescribed for his high blood pressure. At fifty-seven, he looked at least ten years older. By the following year, however, he was looking and feeling much better.

Helping an Old Friend

In the midst of this physical and emotional roller-coaster, Hemingway had the chance to redeem himself for a past unkindness to a friend. Ezra Pound, the brilliant poet who had mentored Hemingway in Paris, was in trouble. After making controversial political remarks, Pound had been accused of treason by the U.S. government. Because of his unstable psychological condition, the poet was placed in a mental hospital. In the summer of 1957, a group of influential poets and authors, including Robert Frost, T. S. Eliot, and Archibald MacLeish, campaigned loudly to have the charges dropped. Although he was too weak to join them in Washington, D.C., Hemingway wrote a long, persuasive letter on Ezra Pound's behalf, explaining why he did not believe Pound was a traitor to his country. As a result, the U.S. Department of Justice finally agreed to release the aging literary giant. Once, in Paris long ago, Hemingway had been on the brink of publicly satirizing his friend. He had now been able to use his writing talent to help him, instead.

By the fall of 1957, Hemingway had found a writing project that kept him occupied for nearly a year. A memoir of his Paris years, it gave him the opportunity to take a second look at his past, to make sense of it, and even to rewrite it in a way that made him feel better about some of the mistakes he had made. In 1958, bringing the manuscript of his memoirs along, he and Mary headed for their favorite hideaway, a vacation home in Ketchum, Idaho, near the ski resort of Sun Valley. As he wrote, his health and good humor steadily improved. Happily, Mary Hemingway wrote to friends that her husband was feeling like his old self again. But Hemingway's momentary redemption could not save him from a final fall.

6 Self-Destruction

Although he wanted to seem indestructible, almost larger than life, the last few years of Ernest Hemingway's life would prove that he was as vulnerable as any other human being. These years were a time of loss of power and control for a man who prized those qualities above all else. The physical deterioration caused by his injuries and his later bouts of reckless drinking and partying took their toll on his productivity. His concern about his ability to work triggered a final, massive depression. The man whose life's goal was to remain undefeated forgot how to go the distance. The despair he had struggled with all his life finally overtook him. But his voice endured in the published and unpublished work he left behind.

While he was still dutifully following doctors' orders to lay off liquor, live quietly, and eat right, Hemingway put finishing touches on the memoir of his Paris years. The idea had been sparked after the Hemingways stopped at the Ritz Hotel in Paris back in 1956. In the hotel's basement, two old trunks belonging to Ernest Hemingway had been gathering dust since 1928. The trunks contained books, sweatshirts, sandals, newspaper clippings, and to the author's great pleasure, stacks of typewritten fiction and blue and yellow notebooks filled with his own handwriting. He told Mary that seeing his writing efforts from so long ago cheered him up, because they made clear to him that it was just as hard for him to write something that pleased him then as it was later. If he had struggled through the blocks then, he could struggle through again. It was never easy, but there was always more to write.

Ernest's lifetime of reckless behavior and binge drinking began to take its toll on the aging writer. He was told by his doctors to start eating right and stop drinking and, for a while, he complied.

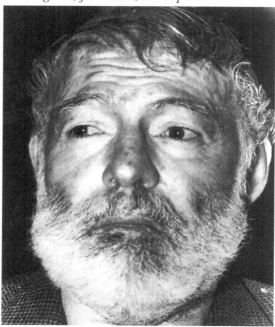

The find had also delighted Hemingway because it brought back his Paris memories with clarity and richness, as though they were happening all over again. According to biographer James R. Mellow: "[The suitcases] were a time capsule from the Paris years. . . . Hemingway, quite probably, would have written his story of the Paris years even if the memorabilia had never been found."[69] Hemingway had never wanted anyone else to write his biography while he was living. But as early as 1949 he had discussed with his publisher the possibility of writing a memoir. The timely recovery of the old trunks had given him an excuse to get started. Now, although the memoir was not destined to be published until after his death, his return to the Paris of his youth with the perspective of maturity had become a reality.

A Moveable Feast

The memoir, eventually titled *A Moveable Feast,* was a series of sketches, or brief scenes, of the young writer's life on the Left Bank of Paris between 1921 and 1926. According to Carlos Baker, Hemingway boasted that the memoir contained "the true gen [short for the true intelligence] on what everyone has written about and no-one knows but me."[70] Even though his memory for names and dates was not as good as it once had been, a fascinating, romantic picture puzzle began to fall into place of the days when he had mingled with the experimental writers, painters, composers, architects, and scholars who had shaped the future direction of the world of arts and letters. The memoir is alive with details of the cultural movement Hemingway had invaded as a cocky, yet idealistic, young talent.

Although it was enormously entertaining, a lot of Hemingway's narratives were unkind portraits of people long dead—he portrays old friends like Gertrude Stein and F. Scott Fitzgerald as pathetic, even repulsive. For example, in his written remembrances of his former mentor, Gertrude Stein, Ernest sarcastically comments: "In the three or four years that we were good friends I cannot remember Gertrude Stein ever speaking well of any writer who had not written favorably about her work or done something to advance her career."[71] Elsewhere he scornfully describes an argument he overheard between Stein and her friend Alice B. Toklas: "I swallowed the drink and put the glass down on the table and started for the door. . . . [Toklas's attacks were] bad to hear and the answers were worse."[72]

Ernest was equally ruthless in his comments about his friend F. Scott Fitzgerald, focusing on the alcoholism and neuroses Scott himself had made no secret of in his own autobiographical writings:

> Scott would resolve not to go on all-night drinking parties and to get some exercise each day and work regularly. He would start to work and as soon as he was working well [his wife] Zelda would begin complaining about how bored she was and get him off on another drunken party. They would quarrel and then make up and he would sweat out the alcohol on long walks with me, and make up his mind that this time he would really work, and would start off well. Then it would start all over again.[73]

The memoir gave Hemingway a chance to reinvent one of the periods of his life he felt most uncomfortable about—his divorce from Hadley. His once-beloved Pauline is described as a scheming rich woman responsible for the death of his first marriage. In fact, Ernest portrayed his relationship with Hadley in glowing terms, even when he had already been unfaithful. He describes Hadley waiting for him at the train station in the ski resort where they were staying. He had just returned from a secret meeting with his new mistress, Pauline: "When I saw my wife again standing by the tracks as the train came in by the piled logs at the station, I wished I had died before I ever loved anyone but her. She was smiling, the sun on her lovely face tanned by the snow and sun." [74] Throughout his life, Ernest had never lost his affection for his first wife. Even after Hadley's remarriage, he kept in touch with her regularly. But in his memoir, he seemed to be trying to release himself from the old guilt and shame he had felt at divorcing her.

Trouble in Cuba

By the summer of 1958, Hemingway had completed about eighteen biographical sketches. The Paris memoirs had taken about a year to write. Meanwhile, Hemingway's beloved Cuba was changing. While the Hemingways relaxed in Ketchum, revolution simmered back home in Cuba. The West increasingly heard of the disturbing escapades of a rebel named Fidel Castro. Hemingway followed the violent uprisings in Cuba, wondering whether he should leave Finca Vigía for good. His personal possessions, to say nothing of his good memories, were still at the farm. Disturbed, he wrote to his son Patrick about the situation:

> Cuba is really bad now, Mouse . . . living in a country where no one is right—both sides atrocious—knowing what sort of stuff and murder will go on when the new ones come in—seeing the abuses of those in now—I am fed on it [sic]. . . . Might pull out of there. Future looks very bad and there has been no fishing in Gulf for 2 years—and will be eventually no freedom coastwise and all the old places ruined. [75]

Even though he worried about Cuba's volatile politics, in Ketchum Ernest found the cherished freedom he craved. He went duck, partridge, and pheasant hunting daily. Mary went along. His health began to flourish at last.

In 1958, Hemingway felt energized enough to meet with a church group of about forty Catholic teens in nearby Hailey, Idaho. The parish priest had asked him to host a question-and-answer session. Evidently, the young people wanted to interview their famous neighbor. As a rule, Hemingway hated public speaking. Reluctantly, though, he told Father O'Connor he would talk to them.

Journalist Aaron Hotchner was a guest of the Hemingways at the time. He attended the meeting and published the interview transcript in an issue of *This Week* later that year. In *Papa Hemingway,* he describes Hemingway's stage fright before the meeting: "Ernest fretted about it every day. He fretted about his throat, which he was sure was conking out, he fretted about not being able to talk at the kids' level, and fretted that they probably knew more about his stuff than he did." [76]

The dreaded talk turned out to be a hit. Hemingway offered some solid advice on writing. He was funny and surprisingly humble. At one point, Hemingway made an honest, if simplified, observation about his writing style: "In stating as fully as I could how things really were, it was often very difficult and I wrote awkwardly and the awkwardness is what they called my style."[77] The students, struggling with writing projects of their own, must have taken comfort in that comment.

The Dangerous Summer

Unfortunately, Hemingway's health plunged after the couple returned to Madrid, where

---

"Take Command of Your Fears"

An excerpt from a rare interview Hemingway granted in the late 1950s to a group of forty high school students in Hailey, Idaho. In addition to answering questions about such practical things as how long it takes to write a book, he discussed larger issues such as the development of his style and confronting the fear of failure. This selection is taken from A. E. Hotchner's Papa Hemingway.

"Q: Have you ever had a failure?
A: You fail every day if you're not going good. When you first start writing you never fail. You think it's wonderful and you have a fine time. You think it's easy to write and you enjoy it very much, but you are thinking of yourself, not the reader. He does not enjoy it very much. Later, when you have learned to write for the reader, it is no longer easy to write. In fact, what you ultimately remember about anything you've written is how difficult it was to write it.

Q: When you were young and first writing, were you frightened of criticism?
A: There was nothing to be afraid of. In the beginning I was not making any money at it and I just wrote as well as I could. I believed in what I wrote—if they didn't like it, it was their fault, they would learn to like it later. But I was really not concerned with criticism and not in close touch with it. When you first start writing you are not noticed—that is the blessing of starting.

Q: Do you ever anticipate failure?
A: If you anticipate failure you'll have it. Of course, you are aware of what will happen if you fail, and you plan your escape routes—you would be unintelligent if you didn't—but you don't anticipate failure in the thing you do. Now I don't want you to think I've never been spooked, but if you don't take command of your fears, no attack will ever go."

When Hemingway returned to Spain to write an article about bullfighting for Life *magazine, he fell back into his bad habits and his health deteriorated.*

the writer needed to complete his research for the *Life* magazine bullfight article he was still working on. Spain's two most celebrated matadors, Antonio Ordoñez and Luis Miguel Dominguin, were vying for the title of world champion bullfighter. This time, when Hemingway went to Spain, the international media followed. Newspapers wanted to cover the showdown between the rival bullfighters, but they were also eager to catch a glimpse of the famous fan. Hemingway's own fans crowded around him. Matadors dedicated bulls to him. Photographers took pictures of him at the bullring and in the cafés.

At Pamplona, the author was surrounded by admiring college students who had read *The Sun Also Rises*. The students identified with the characters, the cynical young adults who were labeled "The Lost Generation," even though Hemingway was sorry he had ever heard Gertrude Stein's phrase or repeated it. Hemingway's pride

was massaged by the publicity. It reassured him that he was still important, still interesting to people. But the late hours and his heavy drinking had serious consequences. Pain flared again in the kidney he had ruptured in the African plane crash.

Hemingway saw his doctor for the kidney trouble. But he did not stop partying. He wanted to have some fun after all the work he had done to recover from his injuries and health problems. And more than anything, he wanted to drink. According to biographer Bernice Kert:

Ernest averaged three hours of sleep a night, rarely even bothering to return to his room but curling up in the front seat of [his rented] Ford. There were seldom fewer than twenty friends—or strangers—at mealtime, with Ernest footing the bill. His massive head with its white beard rose above the crowds who constantly pressed in on him. The

Hemingway ignored his doctor's orders and returned to the all-night drinking binges that had taken a devastating toll on his health.

curly white locks were combed forward to hide his baldness. He drank for hours at a stretch.[78]

Hemingway at Sixty

His sixtieth birthday was coming up. Mary was enthusiastic about making it a celebration to remember. She arranged for target-shooting booths, guitar players, flamenco dancers, Japanese lanterns, fireworks. She spent weeks organizing the big event. Guests came from all over the world. Hemingway and his friends had a wild time. But he did not take the time to thank Mary for it. In the days that followed, Hemingway's behavior got worse. He was horribly rude to Mary, as he had been rude to Martha

Gellhorn years before. He picked fights with her. According to Mellow: "Hemingway accused Mary of spending his money for the party, although she had paid for most of it with an article she had written for *Sports Illustrated*. His moods were becoming volatile. He would start a harangue over minor things. . . . Sometimes arguments would continue on into the small hours of the morning."[79]

Mary left Spain early to get their Cuba and Ketchum homes ready for a visit from Antonio Ordoñez and his wife. But she did not leave happy. She wrote to Hemingway, who had stayed behind in Madrid, that she would be perfectly willing to live separately from him if that was what he wanted. His behavior was pushing her away, she told him. Hemingway tried to make up for hurting her by bringing home a diamond pin as a peace offering. Mary accepted the pin, but she would have preferred to have her loving husband back. She missed the years when the writing of *The Old Man and the Sea* was humming along and Hemingway had been at peace with himself and the world.

Hemingway was always happiest, and easiest to get along with, when his writing was going well. Fortunately, Hemingway's unpleasant behavior calmed down when he returned to Idaho and to his regular writing habits. The fresh air and discipline helped him get back to work. The only problem, in fact, was that it seemed he could not stop writing. His bullfight article for *Life* was now far too long. The manuscript had swollen to 110,000 words. With Aaron Hotchner's editorial help, Hemingway managed to cut the article down to 60,000 words and submitted it to *Life*. Hemingway's lack of control over the length of the piece showed an uncharacteristic lack of professionalism that was a hint of trouble to come. The magazine accepted the article, but had to cut the material further to fit it into their pages. The three "Dangerous Summer" articles appeared in *Life* in 1960, and readers responded enthusiastically.

Cuban Crisis

That frantic bout of writing was only a temporary relief from the dark gloom that was to follow. Ernest and Mary had returned to their farm in San Francisco de Paula. The frightening Cuban revolution was in full swing. Hemingway and other Americans had once sympathized with Castro, thinking he was pro-democracy. But Castro soon denounced the United States and declared he was a Communist. Hemingway's loyalties were torn between the two countries. He hated to abandon Finca Vigía for good. It was the place where he had written the most and the best, for a significant stretch of his writing career. The bristling relations between the United States and Cuba disturbed him in other ways. He had been photographed kissing Castro's flag. Would people see him as a Castro supporter? He convinced himself that the FBI was investigating him because of his connections to Cuba. Soon, he was darting looks over his shoulder everywhere he went.

In the midst of these worries, Hemingway began to brood over financial matters, just as his father had done not long before shooting himself. Hemingway was horrified to learn that his Irish secretary had not renewed her visitor's visa. Even though officials reassured him the oversight was a minor one, Hemingway was positive he would be dragged off to prison for his role in the error. His increasing anxiety was out of all proportion to the situation.

Breakdown in Spain

In the fall of 1960, while Mary waited at home in Ketchum, Hemingway flew back to Spain to scout out photographs to include in a book-length version of "The Dangerous Summer" to be published by Scribner's. This time, he did not enjoy his visit. Instead, his letters during the two-month ordeal showed how severely depressed he felt. On September 23, he wrote Mary that he was not sleeping and that he wished she would come and take care of him and keep him from "cracking up." On September 25, he wrote her again: "Must get out of this and back to you and healthy life in Ketchum and get head in shape to write well."[80] Ernest could not seem to cheer up. The friends he was staying with found him touchy, sad, and irrational. He accused his friend Bill Davis of trying to drive him off a cliff. He spent his last four days in Spain huddled in bed.

When Hemingway made it back home, his wife and friends could see how despondent and anxious he was. Mary, who was used to Hemingway behaving strangely, finally decided that he needed to see a psychiatrist. The only trouble was getting Hemingway to agree to go. He insisted he did not need to see a "head doctor," and he dreaded the bad publicity if word got out. On November 30, however, he agreed to be hospitalized for psychiatric treatment at the Mayo Clinic in Rochester, Minnesota, as long as secrecy could be maintained. He checked in under the name of George

"Woke Bad Today"

In 1960, on a trip to Spain, Hemingway's depression worsened. In Ernest Hemingway: A Life Story, *scholar Carlos Baker reconstructs Hemingway's nightmarish descent into melancholy while staying with friends, the Davises.*

"The Davises had seen him in most of his moods, but none like this. He showed the symptoms of extreme nervous depression: fear, loneliness, ennui, suspicion of the motives of others, insomnia, guilt, remorse, and failure of memory. He had been in Spain only ten days when his letters to his wife complained of cramps and nightmares. At the end of two weeks he said flatly that he feared a 'complete physical and nervous crack up from deadly overwork.' It had been his lifelong habit to awaken cheerfully. Now each day seemed like a nightmare seventy-two hours long. 'Woke bad today,' he said on the 19th. Although he spoke of being lonely, new faces made him nervous. The whole bullfight business seemed 'corrupt' and 'unimportant.'. . . When the first installment of 'The Dangerous Summer' reached him by airmail early in September, he recoiled in anguish at the grinning cover portrait, calling it a 'horrible face.' He felt 'ashamed and sick' to have done such a job, and was full of remorse at having made 'such a mess.' He wrote Mary repeatedly . . . saying that he now realized why she had hated Spain so much in the summer of 1959. He wished that she were with him now to keep him from 'cracking up.'"

Saviers, his personal physician, and pretended to the outside world that he was being treated for high blood pressure.

The Mayo Clinic

The Mayo Clinic doctors recognized his paranoia and depression. Knowing that reserpine, the blood pressure medicine he had been taking, could cause depression, they ordered him to stop taking it. When Hemingway continued to be anxious and irrational, however, they administered shock treatments, a common therapy at the time for mental illness.

Although he was on his best behavior with the Mayo Clinic doctors, Hemingway grumbled privately to Hotchner, "What these shock doctors don't know is about writers and such things as remorse and contrition and what they do to them. They should make all psychiatrists take a course in creative writing so they know about writers."[81] The guilty emotions Hemingway mentioned are common feelings during a depression. Hemingway may have wanted to believe that the mental anguish that had dogged him all his life was also the springboard of his finest writing. But he also seemed to fear that the same anguish that may have inspired him might also destroy him somehow.

Although Hemingway's wife and friends, and perhaps Ernest himself, did not believe that he was getting the relief he needed from his anxiety, the doctors decided to release him on January 22, 1961. Always good at role-playing, he had told them what they wanted to hear. They felt it was a good sign that he had expressed an interest in getting back to work. Back in Ketchum, Hemingway sat down to work every morning. But,

to his increasing despair, the words would no longer come. Asked to contribute to a volume of tributes to President John F. Kennedy, Hemingway spent a week laboring over a four-line statement.

A Dry Well

Hemingway's work meant everything to him. Many times in his life, he had experienced dry spells, often after completing a major project. But, as he explained to journalist George Plimpton in an interview years before, he had always been able to dip once more into the wellspring of his talent and keep writing: "The well is where your 'juice' is. Nobody knows what it is made of, least of all yourself. What you

In addition to his deteriorating mental and physical health, Hemingway was finding it more and more difficult to write. The creative dry spell made him sink even deeper into depression.

know is if you have it, or you have to wait for it to come back."[82] In his time of greatest thirst, Hemingway had rushed to the well and found it bone-dry. Unfortunately, he would not follow his own advice about waiting for it to refill itself.

He confided his hopelessness to Aaron Hotchner, asking bitterly, "'What does a man care about? Staying healthy. Working good. Eating and drinking with his friends. Enjoying himself in bed. I haven't any of them. Do you understand, goddamnit? None of them.'"[83] Hemingway believed that he had lost control over everything in his life that had brought him happiness. His depression was affecting his ability to think reasonably, and he could see no way out of the mental pit he had fallen into.

On April 21, just before Dr. Saviers's scheduled visit, Mary found her sixty-one-year-old husband standing near the front door holding a shotgun in one hand, the shells to load it with in the other. She talked to him for fifty minutes, desperately stalling for time until Dr. Saviers arrived. They eased the gun away from Hemingway and drove him to the hospital in Sun Valley. From there, he was transferred by plane back to Rochester and the Mayo Clinic. But after only a few weeks, the doctors released him again. Mary could see how sad and worried Hemingway still was, but the doctors apparently were fooled. Against her better judgment, she brought him back home to Ketchum. On Sunday, July 2, 1961, Mary woke up to what sounded like a bureau drawer slamming shut. Hem-

"Good Luck, Papa"

A. E. Hotchner, a journalist who befriended Hemingway in his later years, published a book about him after the author's death. The book discusses Hemingway's final bouts of depression and his suicide. In this excerpt from Papa Hemingway, *Hotchner writes about his grief over his friend's death and how he said good-bye.*

"I sent Mary a long cable, but I did not go to Ketchum for the funeral. I could not say good-bye to Ernest in a public group. Instead I went to Santa Maria Sopra Minerva—his church, not mine—because I wanted to say good-bye to him in his own place. I found a deserted side altar and sat there for a long while, thinking about all the good times we had had, remembering forward from the first tentative meeting at the Floridita in Havana. But when it came time to go, all I could think of to say was, Good luck, papa. I figured he knew how much I loved him, so there was no point in mentioning that. I lit a candle and put some money in the poor box and spent the rest of the night alone, wandering through Rome's old streets.

Ernest had had it right: Man is not made for defeat. Man can be destroyed but not defeated."

After a previous suicide attempt and a brief stay at the Mayo Clinic for psychiatric treatment, Ernest Hemingway fatally shot himself in his home in Ketchum, Idaho, on July 2, 1961.

ingway had pressed his double-barreled shotgun against his forehead and pulled the trigger.

Ernest Hemingway once told Lillian Ross that death was "the only thing he knew that was really worthless."[84] He was a fighter who believed in experiencing life to the fullest. The belief that humans can be destroyed physically, but never defeated spiritually if they refuse to give in, was one he carried with him throughout his career. Despite his dark moods, he not only kept enduring, but delivered the world a fine and inspiring body of work. What, then, caused Ernest, at a low point in his life, to let go and take his own life?

Why Suicide?

It may have been that he despaired of ever writing again. After his shock treatments, when the words just would not come, he doubted that he would ever regain his cherished ability to write. To Hemingway, writing was almost as important as breath-

ing. Although it was probably the depression itself causing his writer's block, he told those close to him that he was sure the shock treatments had damaged his mind, destroying his ability to write forever.

A life without writing was daunting for Hemingway to contemplate. Tragically, he did not ride out the rough time and wait to find out whether the words would return. As depression had impaired a father's judgment years earlier, it now affected his son's. As a young soldier experiencing death up close for the first time, Hemingway had written his family that he would rather die young than to die with his "body worn out and old and illusions shattered."[85] At the time of his suicide, his "illusions" about the positive things in life—or perhaps his faith in himself and God—seemed indeed to have disintegrated.

A Family Illness?

Ernest Hemingway was a man who fought the life-threatening illness of depression

The Hemingway family has a tragic history of depression and suicide. In addition to Ernest and his father, two of Ernest's siblings died by their own hand.

all his life while consistently producing some of the best literature of all time. Ernest's father was not the only member of the family who suffered repeated episodes of depression that ended in suicide. Ernest's brother, too, died by his own hand, and one of his sisters committed suicide as well. In 1996, one of his granddaughters, Margaux Hemingway, a model and actress, was found dead at the age of forty-one. She had suffered from epilepsy, alcoholism, and bulimia, an eating disorder. Friends suspected her death, too, might have been a suicide. Ernest himself had suffered his first serious bout with the mental illness as

early as 1919, when he took to his bed after Agnes von Kurowsky rejected him. Depression can be treated—it does not have to end in tragedy, the way it apparently did for so many members of Hemingway's family.

Whatever its source, Ernest bore the weight of the disease bravely, carrying on under its crushing pressure to create an impressive body of work. In a 1938 preface to a collection of his short stories, with some of his greatest works yet ahead of him, he wrote, "I would like to live long enough to write three more novels and twenty-five more stories. I know some pretty good ones." [86]

The Hemingway Legacy

Ernest Hemingway's reputation as a man of action won him attention in his day, but history will remember him for his fiction. His tough, direct style reshaped the way today's writers tell stories. And his work dealt with themes that continue to touch audiences—how to fight fear with courage, how to love a universe that seems indifferent, how to endure life's burdens with dignity. Because life in any time is hard, the aggressive yet sensitive Hemingway hero who sets out to make it through with decency and style has attracted readers through the years and across generations.

After his death, Hemingway's legacy continued. In 1964, three years after he killed himself, *A Moveable Feast* appeared in bookstores. The beautifully written, mocking, bittersweet memoir's publication sparked a wave of curiosity about the Paris arts scene of the 1920s, especially about Hemingway and his contemporaries. Even after he was gone, Hemingway was still "cool," a fact that probably would have pleased him enormously. The book's title is drawn from a line in *Across the River and into the Trees,* in which happiness is described as a moveable feast. (Moveable feasts are religious holidays that are celebrated on a different day each year, such as Easter.)

The next posthumous work to appear in print was *Islands in the Stream,* published in 1970. Mary Hemingway collaborated with Charles Scribner Jr. (Hemingway's publisher) and scholar Carlos Baker to meld three loosely connected narratives together in book form. Set in the Caribbean, they tell the story of a painter named Thomas Hudson. Hemingway's exciting action scenes and expert descriptions of deep-sea fishing drew from his World War II days of scouting submarines from the deck of the *Pilar.* Like *A Moveable Feast* before it, the book was a bestseller.

Sixteen years later a puzzling new Hemingway novel was published after undergoing heavy editing. Hemingway had been working sporadically on *The Garden of Eden* since 1946, taking it up and putting it aside again until his death. He had apparently never felt the sprawling work was ready for publication. The story of an obsessive romance between a writer, his wife, and their friend Marita is set in Mediterranean France and Spain.

A Continuing Fascination

Islands in the Stream and *The Garden of Eden* would probably never have been published during Hemingway's lifetime. He would not have allowed it. But even in raw,

Hemingway's early death did not tarnish the immense literary legacy he left behind. His attention to detail and his simple style are still an inspiration to writers today.

unfinished form, they were welcomed by a public that continues to be fascinated by his work.

An unmistakable part of Hemingway's power is his writing style. His choppy sentences, tough talk, and simple descriptions of natural details brand him as unique. That distinction was part of what he strived for. The powerful language patterns that made his work touch people's feelings also

made it enjoyable to read. Even in the earliest days of his success, his rivals could not resist mimicking him.

Today people continue to flatter him with imitation. In 1978, Harry's Bar & Grill in Key West, Florida, began sponsoring its Imitation Hemingway Competition in his honor. The humorous parodies knock the macho Hemingway hero off his high horse and place him in absurd situations. The language is more Hemingway than Hemingway himself, sprinkled with "ands" and "buts" and shunning commas relentlessly. Hemingway's son John (Bumby) was a judge for the hilarious competition, which received prominent media attention during its eleven years of existence.

Silly contests are not the only way in which Hemingway has invaded public consciousness. Numerous organizations revolving around the appreciation of Hemingway's life, voice, and message have sprung up in the past three decades, including The Ernest Hemingway Foundation of Oak Park. Oak Park also boasts The Hemingway Museum. There are also several scholarly journals devoted to Hemingway's work, including *The Hemingway Review*. In recent years, the World Wide Web has teemed with Hemingway websites.

The myths Hemingway created about himself—ladies' man, fighting machine, heroic survivor—pale when compared to the life story of a real man who struggled to make it through each day. That ordinary man created extraordinary stories. Reading them is perhaps the best way to know him.

Notes

Chapter 1: Origins of a Writer

1. Quoted in Marcelline Hemingway Sanford, *At the Hemingways: A Family Portrait*. Boston: Little, Brown, 1961.

2. Quoted in Bernice Kert, *The Hemingway Women*. New York: W. W. Norton, 1983.

3. Sanford, *At the Hemingways*.

4. Quoted in Ina Mae Schleden and Marion Rawls Herzog, eds., *Ernest Hemingway as Recalled by His High School Contemporaries*. Oak Park, IL: The Historical Society of Oak Park and River Forest, 1973.

5. Quoted in Carlos Baker, *Ernest Hemingway: A Life Story*. New York: Scribner's, 1969.

6. Quoted in Schleden and Herzog, eds., *Ernest Hemingway as Recalled*.

7. Sanford, *At the Hemingways*.

8. Quoted in Baker, *Ernest Hemingway: A Life Story*.

9. Joseph M. Flora, *Ernest Hemingway: A Study of the Short Fiction*. Boston: Twayne, 1989.

10. Quoted in Matthew J. Bruccoli, ed., *Ernest Hemingway, Cub Reporter: Kansas City Star Stories*. Pittsburgh: University of Pittsburgh Press, 1970.

11. Quoted in Henry S. Villard and James Nagel, *Hemingway in Love and War: The Lost Diary of Agnes von Kurowsky*. Boston: Northeastern University Press, 1989.

12. Quoted in Villard and Nagel, *Hemingway in Love and War*.

13. Quoted in Baker, *Ernest Hemingway: A Life Story*.

14. Quoted in Villard and Nagel, *Hemingway in Love and War*.

15. Quoted in Schleden and Herzog, eds., *Ernest Hemingway as Recalled*.

16. Quoted in Richard O'Connor, *Ernest Hemingway*. New York: McGraw-Hill, 1971.

17. Kert, *The Hemingway Women*.

18. Quoted in Harold Bloom, ed., *Ernest Hemingway*. New York: Chelsea House, 1985.

19. Sanford, *At the Hemingways*.

Chapter 2: Writer First

20. Ernest Hemingway, *A Moveable Feast*. New York: Scribner's, 1964.

21. Flora, *Ernest Hemingway*.

22. Quoted in Baker, *Ernest Hemingway: A Life Story*.

23. Ernest Hemingway, *By-Line: Ernest Hemingway*, ed. William White. New York: Scribner's, 1967.

24. Quoted in Kert, *The Hemingway Women*.

25. Quoted in Baker, *Ernest Hemingway: A Life Story*.

26. Quoted in Baker, *Ernest Hemingway: A Life Story*.

27. Hemingway, *A Moveable Feast*.

28. Hemingway, *A Moveable Feast*.

29. Quoted in Ernest Hemingway, *The Hemingway Reader*, ed., Charles Poore. New York: Scribner's, 1953.

30. Quoted in Bruccoli, ed., *Ernest Hemingway, Cub Reporter*.

31. Quoted in Flora, *Ernest Hemingway*.

32. Hemingway, *By-Line: Ernest Hemingway*.

33. Ernest Hemingway, *The Sun Also Rises*. New York: Scribner's, 1995.

Chapter 3: Defending Champion

34. Sanford, *At the Hemingways.*

35. Quoted in Carlos Baker, ed., *Ernest Hemingway: Selected Letters 1917–1961.* New York: Scribner's, 1981.

36. Quoted in Sanford, *At the Hemingways.*

37. Kert, *The Hemingway Women.*

38. Michael Reynolds, *Hemingway: The 1930s.* New York: W. W. Norton, 1997.

39. Reynolds, *Hemingway: The 1930s.*

40. Ernest Hemingway, *A Farewell to Arms.* New York: Scribner's, 1995.

41. Reynolds, *Hemingway: The 1930s.*

42. Quoted in Baker, *Ernest Hemingway: A Life Story.*

43. Ernest Hemingway, *Death in the Afternoon.* New York: Scribner's, 1932.

44. Quoted in Baker, *Ernest Hemingway: A Life Story.*

45. Quoted in Baker, *Ernest Hemingway: A Life Story.*

46. Quoted in Baker, ed., *Ernest Hemingway: Selected Letters.*

47. O'Connor, *Ernest Hemingway.*

Chapter 4: Self-Absorption

48. Quoted in Baker, *Ernest Hemingway: A Life Story.*

49. Reynolds, *Hemingway: The 1930s.*

50. Ernest Hemingway, *For Whom the Bell Tolls.* New York: Scribner's, 1995.

51. Reynolds, *Hemingway: The 1930s.*

52. Quoted in Matthew J. Bruccoli, *Fitzgerald and Hemingway.* New York: Carroll and Graf, 1994.

53. Baker, *Ernest Hemingway: A Life Story.*

54. Katie de Koster, ed., *Readings on Ernest Hemingway.* San Diego: Greenhaven Press, 1997.

55. Quoted in Kert, *The Hemingway Women.*

56. Quoted in Kert, *The Hemingway Women.*

57. Kert, *The Hemingway Women.*

58. Baker, *Ernest Hemingway: A Life Story.*

59. Quoted in James R. Mellow, *A Life Without Consequences.* Boston: Houghton Mifflin, 1992.

Chapter 5: Redemption

60. Ernest Hemingway, *The Old Man and the Sea.* New York: Scribner's, 1995.

61. Hemingway, *The Old Man and the Sea.*

62. Quoted in Baker, *Ernest Hemingway: A Life Story.*

63. Quoted in Bloom, ed., *Ernest Hemingway.*

64. Quoted in Mellow, *A Life Without Consequences.*

65. Baker, *Ernest Hemingway: A Life Story.*

66. Quoted in Mellow, *A Life Without Consequences.*

67. Quoted in Baker, *Ernest Hemingway: A Life Story.*

68. Quoted in Kert, *The Hemingway Women.*

Chapter 6: Self-Destruction

69. Mellow, *A Life Without Consequences.*

70. Quoted in Baker, *Ernest Hemingway: A Life Story.*

71. Hemingway, *A Moveable Feast.*

72. Hemingway, *A Moveable Feast.*

73. Hemingway, *A Moveable Feast.*

74. Hemingway, *A Moveable Feast.*

75. Quoted in Baker, ed., *Ernest Hemingway: Selected Letters.*

76. A. E. Hotchner, *Papa Hemingway.* New York: Bantam Books, 1967.

77. Quoted in Hotchner, *Papa Hemingway.*

78. Kert, *The Hemingway Women.*

79. Mellow, *A Life Without Consequences.*

80. Quoted in Baker, ed., *Ernest Hemingway: Selected Letters.*

81. Hotchner, *Papa Hemingway.*

82. Quoted in Bloom, ed., *Ernest Hemingway.*

83. Quoted in Hotchner, *Papa Hemingway.*

84. Quoted in Lillian Ross, *Reporting.* New York: Simon and Schuster, 1964.

85. Quoted in Baker, ed., *Ernest Hemingway: Selected Letters.*

86. Ernest Hemingway, *The Short Stories of Ernest Hemingway.* New York: Scribner's, 1938.

For Further Reading

Books About Hemingway

Carlos Baker, *Ernest Hemingway: A Life Story*. New York: Scribner's, 1969. Spanning six decades, this massive yet readable biography is the first definitive book about Hemingway's life and remains the standard reference work. Carlos Baker is a literature professor who drew form diaries, letters, and unpublished works to paint this sweeping portrait.

Matthew J. Bruccoli, ed., *Ernest Hemingway, Cub Reporter: Kansas City Star Stories*. Pittsburgh: University of Pittsburgh Press, 1970. Presents and analyzes Hemingway's articles for the *Kansas City Star*, his first journalism. Entertaining and insightful look at Hemingway as a young man, and at the roots of his unique style.

Cynthia Maziarka and Donald Vogel Jr., eds., *Hemingway at Oak Park High: The High School Writings of Ernest Hemingway, 1916–1917*. Oak Park, IL: Oak Park and River Forest High School, 1993. Ernest's high school yearbook comments: "None are to be found more clever than Ernie." This small book contains complete transcripts of his articles for the school newspaper and the school literary magazine, as well as articles written about him by Oak Park students after he returned from the war. Reveals the roots of the "Hemingway style." With an introduction by biographer Michael Reynolds.

Richard O'Connor, *Ernest Hemingway*. New York: McGraw-Hill, 1971. A lively retelling of the exciting story of Hemingway's adventures, written for young people. Includes a foreword by biographer Carlos Baker.

Charles Poore, ed., *The Hemingway Reader: Selected with a Foreword and Twelve Brief Prefaces by Charles Poore*. New York: Scribner's, 1953. This anthology contains *The Sun Also Rises* and *The Torrents of Spring* in their entirety, as well as ten stories and selected excerpts from his major books, including *Death in the Afternoon* and *Across the River and into the Trees*.

Lillian Ross, *Reporting*. New York: Simon and Schuster, 1964. A collection of articles by the reporter who interviewed Hemingway for *Life* magazine, including the famous profile of Hemingway and her discussion of it.

Ina Mae Schleden and Marion Rawls Herzog, eds., *Ernest Hemingway as Recalled by His High School Contemporaries*. The Historical Society of Oak Park and River Forest, 1973. A childhood friend of Hemingway's, a high school classmate, the head of the English Department while Ernest attended high school, one of his English teachers, and a student of American literature each wrote a section of this revealing booklet.

Henry S. Villard and James Nagel, *Hemingway in Love and War: The Lost Diary of Agnes von Kurowsky*. Boston: Northeastern University Press, 1989. Tells the story of Hemingway's World War I years, focusing on his relationship with Agnes von Kurowsky, drawing from her diaries and eyewitness accounts.

Books by Hemingway

By-Line: Ernest Hemingway: Selected Articles and Dispatches of Four Decades. Edited by William White. New York: Scribner's, 1967. A large collection of Hemingway's published work in newspapers and magazines between 1920 and 1956 that represents only one-third of his total journalistic output during that time. Includes the magazine account he wrote of his near-fatal plane crashes in Africa in 1954.

Death in the Afternoon. New York: Scribner's, 1932. Hemingway's thoughts on bullfighting, life, and death. Poetic and graphic descriptions of Spanish bullfights, laced with commentary on Hemingway's own contemporaries, including his critics.

A Farewell to Arms. New York: Scribner's, 1995. Hemingway's powerful and moving World War I novel, a tragic love story, was a success in its day and remains a classic story of the inevitability of evil and humanity's attempts to surmount it.

For Whom the Bell Tolls. New York: Scribner's, 1995. Considered by many to be one of Hemingway's greatest books, it chronicles the saga of the Spanish Civil War that preceded World War II. Hemingway drew from his own firsthand experiences as a war correspondent for the events of the novel.

A Moveable Feast. New York: Scribner's, 1964. These vivid, often funny sketches of Hemingway's life in Paris in the 1920s remembered more than three decades later, were published after his death.

The Old Man and the Sea. New York: Scribner's, 1995. Hemingway won the 1953 Pulitzer Prize for Fiction for this brief, haunting novel about an old fisherman trying to bring in a huge marlin, a simply told tale that many believe symbolizes the enduring dignity of man and the necessity for people to rely on God.

The Short Stories of Ernest Hemingway. New York: Scribner's, 1938. A collection of Hemingway's first forty-nine stories, introduced with a brief preface by the author written in 1938. Famous stories include "The Short Happy Life of Francis Macomber," "Indian Camp," and "A Clean, Well Lighted Place."

The Sun Also Rises. New York: Scribner's, 1955. Originally titled "Fiesta," this classic early Hemingway novel explores the emotionally detached behavior of a group of young people at a bullfight fiesta in Pamplona, Spain, whose dreams have been shattered by World War I. Hemingway once considered titling the novel "The Lost Generation." *The Sun Also Rises* was a bestseller, winning praise for its vivid dialogue and tense action.

Works Consulted

Carlos Baker, ed., *Ernest Hemingway: Selected Letters 1917–1961.* New York: Scribner's, 1981. Nearly six hundred letters cast light on Hemingway's life while revealing him to be a witty, enthusiastic letter writer. Selected by Carlos Baker, the author of *Ernest Hemingway: A Life Story.*

Harold Bloom, ed., *Ernest Hemingway.* New York: Chelsea House, 1985. A collection of literary essays and interviews on Hemingway and his work.

Matthew J. Bruccoli, *Fitzgerald and Hemingway.* New York: Carroll and Graf, 1994. A biographical study focusing on the friendship and working relationship of Ernest Hemingway and F. Scott Fitzgerald.

Katie de Koster, ed., *Readings on Ernest Hemingway.* San Diego: Greenhaven Press, 1997. An annotated selection of literary essays about Hemingway's work. Includes a helpful timeline and a summary of the highlights of Hemingway's life story.

Joseph M. Flora, *Ernest Hemingway: A Study of the Short Fiction.* Boston: Twayne, 1989. Literary discussion of Hemingway's short stories, including the Nick Adams stories.

Norberto Fuentes, *Hemingway in Cuba.* Secaucus, NJ: Lyle Stuart, 1984. Written by the son of a friend of Hemingway's when he lived in Cuba, this translation contains an introduction by Gabriel García Márquez. Gives snapshot impressions, through vignettes, of Hemingway's time in Cuba, especially his antics on the *Pilar.*

A. E. Hotchner, *Papa Hemingway.* New York: Bantam Books, 1967. An eyewitness account of Hemingway in his last thirteen years written by a close associate, journalist Aaron Hotchner. Mary Hemingway sued to stop publication of the book, which deals frankly with Hemingway's suicidal depression.

Bernice Kert, *The Hemingway Women.* New York: W. W. Norton, 1983. An excellent, readable analysis of the women in Hemingway's life, from his mother and sisters to his wives, and what they were like as individuals outside the shadow of Hemingway's reputation.

James R. Mellow, *A Life Without Consequences.* Boston: Houghton Mifflin, 1992. A substantial and thoughtful biography of Ernest Hemingway.

Michael Reynolds, *Hemingway: The 1930s.* New York: W. W. Norton, 1997. An excellent volume in a series studying Hemingway's life and work in detail. This volume focuses on the years in which he got involved in big-game hunting and bullfighting, and looks frankly at his marriages to Pauline Pfeiffer and Martha Gellhorn.

Marcelline Hemingway Sanford, *At the Hemingways: A Family Portrait.* New York: Atlantic Monthly Press, 1962. Delightful memoir by Hemingway's older sister, Marcelline. She chronicles everyday family life, including insights into the children's relationship with their parents. Covers Ernest's youth up through his return from World War I. Also includes an account of his return to his parents' home upon the death of his father, and provides insight into Ed Hemingway's state of mind before his suicide.

Index

Picture Credits

Cover photo: National Archives

Alla Capbell/John F. Kennedy Library, 56

Archive Photo, 9, 27, 31, 34, 76, 86

Archive Photo/American Stock, 60, 72, 81

Archive Photo/David Lees, 30

Archive Photo/Express Newspapers, 77, 91

Archive Photo/Lambert, 46, 85

Ernest Hemingway Foundation of Oak Park, 11, 12, 13, 15, 23, 25, 41, 42, 92

FPG International, 22, 38, 55, 58

John Bryson/John F. Kennedy Library, 94

John F. Kennedy Library, 21, 37, 49, 64, 65, 70, 74, 89

Look/John F. Kennedy Library, 73

New York Times/Archive Photo, 48

Popperfoto, 63

About the Author

Paula Bryant Pratt graduated from Reed College and completed her graduate study at San Diego State University. She has been an in-house editor at Harcourt Brace and Company and a freelance author and editor. She has also taught community college English composition and creative writing. She is the author of Lucent Books' *The Importance of Martha Graham, Maps: Plotting Places on the Globe, Architecture, The End of Apartheid in South Africa,* and *The Importance of Jane Goodall.* Paula and her husband, Michael, have a daughter, Cerise Olivia.